NORTH OF THE PYRENEES

by the same author

PORTUGAL
BRITTANY
INTRODUCING THE CHANNEL ISLANDS
THE SPANISH PYRENEES
THE CANARY ISLANDS

North of the Pyrenees

HENRY MYHILL

FABER AND FABER
3 Queen Square
London

First published in 1973
by Faber and Faber Limited
3 Queen Square London WC1
Printed in Great Britain by
Ebenezer Baylis & Son Ltd.
The Trinity Press, Worcester, and London

ISBN 0 571 08671 3

To Freda White,

*to whose books I owe my own introduction to,
and love for south-west France*

ACKNOWLEDGEMENTS

I wish to thank the French Government Tourist Office, 178 Piccadilly, London, for permission to reproduce all the photographs in this book, and Sugar Music, 90 Avenue des Champs-Elysées, Paris, for permission to quote six lines from the song *Siffler sur la Colline*.

For other help I wish to thank Monsieur R. Lapassade of Orthez, poet in his Gascon language, and authority on the history of his native Béarn; Monsieur Ferlin of Montauban; Monsieur André Gaure of Barbaste; Monsieur and Madame Laurens and their daughter, Maryse, of Meilhan; Mr. Cedric Dannatt of Rébénacq; Mrs. Liliane Wingfield of Castetnau; Mr. and Mrs. John Gates; the Lavalette family of Aurensan; and the Directeur of the Musée Pyrénéen at Lourdes.

CONTENTS

Acknowledgements	9
Introduction	15
1 Pays Basque	21
1. *Labourd*	21
2. *Bayonne*	32
3. *Basse-Navarre*	36
4. *Soule*	40
2 Béarn	46
1. *Along the Gaves*	46
2. *Pau*	55
3. *Up the valleys*	65
4. *North of Pau*	75
3 Gascony	79
1. *Armagnac*	79
2. *The Coteaux*	90
3. *Chalosse*	95
4 The Pinelands	99
1. *Landes*	99
2. *Silver Coast*	103
3. *Médoc*	107
5 Bigorre and Comminges	109
1. *Bigorre*	190
2. *High Pyrenees*	114

Contents

3. *Comminges*   120
4. *Couserans*   123

6 County of Foix   128
  1. *The River of Gold*   128
  2. *Petites Pyrénées*   135
  3. *Donézan and Sault*   137

7 Pyrenean Catalonia   139
  1. *Capcir*   139
  2. *Cerdagne*   143
  3. *Conflent*   146
  4. *Vallespir*   153

8 Along the Garonne   158
  1. *Lomagne*   158
  2. *Agenais*   163
  3. *Sauternes*   169

Envoi: *Across the Garonne*   175

Appendix   177
  1. *Getting there*   177
  2. *Settling there*   178
  3. *Eating and sleeping*   180
  4. *Maps*   181

Bibliography   183

Index   185

ILLUSTRATIONS

1   The inner harbour of St-Jean-de-Luz   *following page*   32
2   The Nive near Cambo   32
3   'Discoidal' Basque tombs   32
4   The farms of Béarn have steeply pitched slate roofs   48
5   Basque cross in Soule   48
6   Hastingues   48
7   The arcade frames a street in Bidache   48
8   Salies-de-Béarn: houses of the salt shareholders   48
9   The remains of Sauveterre-de-Béarn's fortified bridge   64
10 The thirteenth-century fortified bridge across the
    Gave at Orthez   64
11 Lescun with its *cirque*   72
12 The tiny fortified village of Larressingle   72
13 The geese of Gascony   72
14 Tapping the resin in the Landes on the traditional
    stilts   72
15 The lake of Hossegor   72
16 The basket-work *chisteras* in action on the *fronton* of
    Hossegor   72
17 Europe's largest sand-dune: Pyla near Arcachon   80
18 Château Lafite, at the heart of the great vineyards of
    the Haut-Médoc   80
19 Ste-Marie-de-Campan on the upper Adour in Bigorre   80
20 Floating through the caves of Bétharram   80
21 The Pic du Midi de Bigorre   96

Illustrations

22 Looking from the Col de l'Aubisque towards the Pic
    de Ger   *following page* 96
23 Near the Col de Soulor on the *Route des Pyrénées*   96
24 The time-hallowed approach to the Cirque de Gavarnie
    for those who prefer not to walk   96
25 The column of the four Evangelists in the cathedral
    cloister of St-Bertrand-de-Comminges   112
26 The château of Foix   112
27 Roofscape of tiles in Foix   128
28 Corneilla-de-Conflent   128
29 Romanesque capitals and horse-shoe arch at St-Michel-
    de-Cuxa   144
30 Chapel in the Vallespir   144
31 The twin-columned Gothic cloister of the abbey of
    Arles-sur-Tech   160
32 The château of Labrède, family home of Montesquieu   160

INTRODUCTION

Why 'north of the Pyrenees'? To the English reader—and for most Frenchmen too—the region this book aims to describe is seen the other way round.

To those approaching by the Route Nationale 10 it is 'beyond Bordeaux'. They know they have arrived there when, barely beyond the last suburbs, their lungs fill with resin-rich air as around them closes in the immense pine forest of the Landes.

To those approaching by the Route Nationale 20, on the other hand, it lies 'beyond Toulouse'. If they are lucky enough to be travelling at dawn on a clear day, their moment of conscious arrival comes only a few kilometres beyond that rose-red city of brick. It is the moment when they become suddenly aware of a great wall closing the plain of Pamiers: a wall crowned by towers far higher and of a lovelier shade even than those of the great Toulousain churches of the Jacobins and St-Sernin. They are the snow-covered peaks of the Pyrenees, glowing pink in the early morning sun.

Bordeaux and Toulouse lie on the same river, and five-sixths of our region could be described as 'south of the Garonne'. Such a title would bring this guide into line with the three beautiful books by Freda White to which it hopes to serve as the humble complement. For in *Three Rivers of France*, in *West of the Rhône*, and in *Ways of Aquitaine* (which was very nearly published as *South of the Loire*), she used rivers not merely as her boundaries, but as her living framework.

15

But although she extends *West of the Rhône* all the way to Perpignan and Collioure, she stops short of the Pyrenean foothills. The rivers Tech and Tet interest her only after they have escaped on to the plain of Roussillon. Following the Aude upstream she halts at the gorge of Pierre Lys above Quillan. And declaring that 'the road from Carcassonne is the frontier of this book', she ignores the Ariège altogether.

Respectfully, I accept her frontier to the south as my frontier to the north. This leaves me not only everything 'south of the Garonne', but also the old counties of Comminges, of Couserans, and of Foix, the Pays de Sault and the Pyrenean parts of French Catalonia. In terms of modern departments this embraces all of Landes, Pyrénées-Atlantiques, Hautes-Pyrénées, Gers and Ariège; much of Gironde, Lot-et-Garonne, Haute-Garonne and Pyrénées-Orientales; and fractions of Tarn-et-Garonne and Aude.

Geographically their location 'north of the Pyrenees' is the one thing they all have in common. Historically, too, the region should be surveyed from the crest of the mountain chain which dominates it. For though we ourselves may approach it from the north, many of those whose names we most associate with these lands travelled in the opposite direction.

Thus did the legions of the youthful Pompey in 79 B.C. Climbing up from Spain they descended the Somport pass to found on the upper Garonne an earlier and a lusher Lyon: Lugdunum Convenarum, near the modern St-Bertrand-de-Comminges.

Thus did the Basques, that ancient race never fully absorbed by Rome. In the sixth century, after Rome had fallen, they moved north into the vacuum left between defeated Visigoths and over-stretched Franks, to give Gascony the deformation of their own name it still bears.

Thus did the great family who by prudent management of their patrimony, clever marriage alliances, and skilful military leadership, came near to building a Pyrenean state covering most of our region. In turn Viscounts of Béarn, Counts of Foix, and Kings of Navarre, they finally solved the paradox of their position when in 1588 Henry of Navarre led his army across the Garonne, never to return south. For the lands north of the Pyrenees did not become truly French until they placed their own leader on the throne of France.

Thus did Wellington, bursting up through Spain in the autumn of 1813, to invade French provinces which had not seen fighting since the Wars of Religion.

By the same route as my great compatriot, but in more peaceful circumstances, I was lucky enough to enter this region myself. Countless times during long intervals from my work at San Sebastian I drove across the Bidassoa, to breathe a somehow tangier air, to see with somehow clearer vision, the moment I was across the International Bridge. Perhaps it is the French language itself, at once more liquid yet more precise, which sharpens every sensation experienced on Gallic soil. However deep one's love of Spain, a certain muddiness obscures one's thought processes there, just as it colours so many of the Iberian rivers.

It was the purity of the French rivers, by comparison with the polluted streams of the Spanish province of Guipúzcoa, which always impressed me as I drove on north and east. That and their number. Nivelle, Nive and Adour, minor streams with all the self-assurance of the Ebro or the Guadilquivir, in turn dominated the landscape.

For this is a land shaped by rivers, just as surely as those lands described by Freda White beyond the mighty Garonne into which most of them flow. And one characteristic at least is shared by every river we shall cross. They all run north from the Pyrenees.

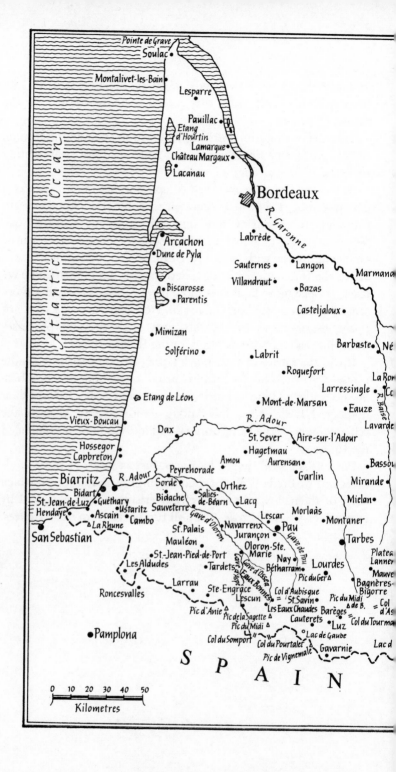

Chapter 1

PAYS BASQUE

1. LABOURD

A few of these rivers, including the Garonne itself, have their sources in Spain, for the frontier does not exactly correspond to the crest of the range. During its first ten miles inland from the Atlantic there is in fact no crest at all. Here the little river Bidassoa divides the two nations before it disappears into Spanish Navarre for the first three-quarters of its life.

It is less than ten years since my work—and often my leisure— used to take me across the International Bridge between Hendaye and Irún as often as several times a week. It seemed busy then. But now there are three such bridges instead of only one, while the alternative frontier post two miles upstream, at Béhobie, has also been enormously extended. For besides being the main road from Paris to Madrid, this is the route followed by most tourists from northern Europe on their way to the west and south of the peninsula.

The number of these has multiplied with the development of the Costa del Sol, and the 'discovery' of Portugal. All too many rush through France, boasting of how they made Spain within twenty-four hours of the Channel or the Rhine. Many are naturally anxious to profit from their annual ration of sunshine by getting as far south as possible as soon as possible. Others, with all their long vacation, or all their retirement ahead of them, have less excuse to press on 'to get through the Customs before the light goes'.

It was not always so. We do not have to go back as far as the three centuries from 1152 to 1451, when Bayonne was second only to Bordeaux as port and commercial centre for the English kings' possessions in south-west France. As recently as between the wars the *Côte Basque* was as fashionable for British visitors as the *Côte d'Azur*.

For the French it still is. The Pyrénées-Atlantiques come immediately after the Riviera departments of the Alpes-Maritimes and the Var in number of summer visitors. And the overwhelming majority of these crowd into the twenty miles of coast between the Bidassoa and the bar of the Adour.

The Briton who pauses at Biarritz or St-Jean-de-Luz for longer than the minutes necessary to quench his thirst before tackling the frontier experiences, therefore, an unusual mixture of actuality with nostalgia. All about him the happy families straight from a *Paris-Match* advertisement, the trim girls direct from the pages of *Elle*, step from their Renaults and Peugeots, or trip down the steps of concrete Casinos. This is the *Cinquième République*, from the neat blue and orange tents of the countless *campings* to the functional furnished flats which have largely replaced the grand hotels.

But a few of those grand hotels still linger, though often converted likewise into apartments. Their façades are not the only relics of the *Côte Basque* of the Third Republic, when panama hats rather than bikinis graced the Port Vieux and the Rue St-Jacques. English churches with attached libraries still minister to decimated Anglo-Saxon colonies, of whose presence one is reminded by the occasional elderly figure in tweed costume. And the happy if passing moment they represent, when English cosiness could be lived against a background of French *douceur de vivre*, lives on in scores of novels of the 'twenties, finding an echo even in Hemingway.

Neither in the 'twenties nor the 'seventies, however, does the image conjured up by the *Côte Basque* seem particularly Basque. This is not because the summer influx of visitors destroys the flavour of indigenous life. A great play is made with the trivia of local folklore and vocabulary. *Chisteiras* for playing pelota are offered for sale alongside the *ambre solaire* and the inflatable boats. Staying in the *Eskalduna* apartments one has a drink at the *Bar Basque*, or a meal at a restaurant with a name like *Etchebertzea*. And French architects, adept at adopting regional styles, have been particularly happy in their transformation of the traditional half-timbered, red-roofed Basque farmhouse into the coquette *villa basque* of the cliffs behind Bidart and Guétary.

The absence nevertheless of a readily recognizable Basque atmosphere is due, I feel, to other reasons. For the English visitor these are above all French resorts, in which he looks for, and finds, the typically French rather than some esoteric peripheral culture. To the Frenchman, on the other hand, this is almost Spain. He is intrigued by the advertisements for bull-fights across the frontier in San Sebastian, and by the coach-loads of eager Spanish shoppers streaming into the department stores of *Biarritz-Bonheur*, or *Aux Dames de France* at Bayonne.

And what do I, who know this coast so well, chiefly remember it for? Not for the galleried Basque churches of St-Jean-de-Luz or Sare. Nor for the strange Basque tombs of the churchyards of Ascain or Ainhoa. Not even for the self-conscious Basque equivalents of *Chez-nous* and *Mon Repos* on the gates of the villas. What I remember best of all is the climate.

In his recent autobiography, *A Late Education*, Alan Moorehead remarks: 'There is a quality of gladness—the *"riant"* of the Guide Bleu and the Baedeker—about the Pays Basque and the Basses-Pyrénées in the early summer that makes you wonder why you waste your time living in any other place.' And of many days that is certainly true, from April all the way through to October. But there is plenty of rain: sometimes whole weeks with nothing else. Nor does this invariably fall in its usual soft drizzle, so aptly named in Basque as *siri-miri*.

For by some meteorological quirk this hilly coast in the right-angle between France and Spain seems to act as a catalyst, sparking off thunder storms. During two summers I rented a studio flat above the Casino of St-Jean-de-Luz, and from its grandstand view would watch fascinated as the lightning flashed over that perfect bay. It was almost as if rockets were being fired from the lighthouse of Socoa and the Pointe-Ste-Barbe which together close it in.

But for all that it was mild. Away from work I never wore a pair of socks all summer. And the rain gave the whole coast a well-washed appearance, making the villas yet more *coquettes*, and the fields between the little white resorts an unfading green. Certainly I, too, was glad those summers to be nowhere else.

I believe the main reason for the lack of an immediately identifiable Basque flavour to be the elusive quality of Basque culture. It is not what we expect it to be. Rodney Gallop, whose *A Book of the Basques* is still the best work on the subject in English, grew up at St-Jean-de-Luz when the *pays basque* was at its most fashionable, and when some of the interest evoked by the country-side had spilled over on to the people who lived there. But he felt that they were subjected to a complete misrepresentation, and wrote his book largely to correct it.

Perhaps it is the climate which makes us imagine them a race not only mysterious, but mystical. The work of concealment carried out by those innumerable hills is supported by the misty atmosphere, which renders rare the days when the natural bel-vedere of La Rhune offers the full extent of its formidable pan-orama. But the Basques are in fact a down-to-earth people of peasant farmers and fishermen. If their practical approach to life is at the same time highly traditional, this is because they have lived in the same area, and in the same style, for a very long time.

Every nation's language tells us a lot about them. But none more so than that of the Basques, which is the oldest in Europe, and whose word for describing themselves is *Euskaradun*, the people of the *Euskara* speech. For it is impossible to express abstractions in this agglutinative tongue, unrelated to any of the Indo-European linguistic family. Even poetry comes grudgingly, when a song which starts by proclaiming 'the pigeon is lovely in the sky' can immediately bring down bird and tone alike by continuing 'and even lovelier on the table'. When the young

Basque terrorists were tried in Burgos in 1970, foreign commentators were wide of the mark in likening their character to that of the Irish, and even using such wild phrases as 'oriental fatalism'.

The Burgos trial reminds us that more than three out of four of the 800,000 Basques live in Spain. These Spanish Basques are at once more numerous, and richer. Not only Bilbao itself, but most of the small towns of Vizcaya and Guipúzcoa have long been hives of industry, and the capital generated has given Basque banking a vital place in the Spanish economy.

There has been no such industrialization north of the Bidassoa. Within France the Basques form an insignificant minority, without political importance or financial power. For this very reason, however, the three French Basque provinces give a clearer idea of how the race lived during the long centuries before industry changed their way of life, and self-conscious nationalism their way of thinking.

Their area is small in relation not only to France, but even to the nine odd departments which form the subject of this book. Together Labourd, Basse-Navarre and Soule cover just over a third of the Pyrénées-Atlantiques, without including its capital Pau, and with only a partial claim on its other big town, Bayonne.

Holding the entire *Côte Basque* within its borders, Labourd is naturally the best-known and the most visited. It is a magic coast, and the visitor need feel no more shame in making its acquaintance before he explores the interior than have I in describing it first. Its magic comes from its Basque background, even when this is misrepresented and popularized; and from its unexpected configuration. For anyone who has been following the French coast meets here the first cliffs since he left Brittany.

The best of these cliffs lie between Hendaye-Plage and Ciboure, and the lovely road along them has with reason been christened the *corniche basque*. But there are others at Guétary and Bidart, and at Biarritz itself. At both its extremities the coast ends in flat sandy promontories, extending between the boundary rivers and the ocean. That alongside the Bidassoa bears the little resort of the 'thirties, Hendaye-Plage. That round which the Adour has flowed since 1578 has a pine forest, a lake called Chiberta, and a cave with the romantic name of the Chambre d'Amour, where a pair of lovers are said to have drowned in the rising tide.

The sea continues to claim its annual toll of victims, although its greatest threat takes the form not of tides but of currents. The Basque beaches are so clean, so vast, and so golden that they invite the taking of risks. The lifeguards at Hendaye-Plage and Biarritz are rightly strict. This is one reason for the ever-increasing popularity of St-Jean-de-Luz, whose perfect semi-circular bay is completely protected by breakwaters.

It would deserve a slow visit even without that safe, firm sand. For at the heart of the not unattractive accretions of *villas basques* and promenade lie not one, but two little Basque fishing towns. The bridge over the river Nivelle which joins them lies immediately upstream from the port which has been carved out of its little estuary. France's largest tunny-fishing fleet crowded there is the true symbol of the town's past and present.

Yet the great historical event of St-Jean-de-Luz was the marriage on 9th June 1660 between Louis XIV and Maria Teresa, daughter of Philip IV of Spain. This followed the signing of the Treaty of the Pyrenees the previous year on the half-French, half-Spanish islet of the Pheasants in the Bidassoa, just below Béhobie. The great rectangular church of St-Jean-Baptiste, where it was celebrated, is more famous for its blocked main door, sealed up after the bridal pair had passed through, than for the magnificent woodwork of its galleried interior. And the two seventeenth-century town houses of Lohobiague and Haramader are celebrated as the lodgings of Louis XIV and his bride rather than as witnesses to an earlier prosperity based on whale and cod.

The town beyond the Nivelle is Ciboure, among whose picturesque back streets I have searched in vain for any lingering remnants of the *cagots*, an 'untouchable' caste in the Basque country who were once particularly numerous here. But the frontal road along the harbour is named Quai Maurice Ravel, after my favourite modern composer who was born in 1875 at Number 12. He had not a drop of Basque blood in his veins, and used the *pays basque* as a listening post where he picked up the inspiration from beyond the Pyrenees for such works as *L'Heure espagnole* and *Boléro*. And he finally settled at Montfort l'Amaury near Paris—an ominous name as we shall find at the other end of the Pyrenees.

Yet Ravel and his music somehow catch the essence of that happy though transitory moment we have already referred to of the *côte basque* between the wars. It was possible then for a new generation in the arts quietly to experiment without disturbing, or even necessarily rejecting, the values of the old.

Ravel quietly composing: Rodney Gallop quietly studying a still-living Basque folklore: 'Palinurus' 'pursuing a mackintosh, a beret and a strand of wet curls round the sea-wall in the rain'; they stand for St-Jean-de-Luz. The figure who stands for the Biarritz of the 'twenties is necessarily more *mondain*. But for all that the Duke of Windsor remained as faithful to this 'queen of resorts' as to the woman for whom he gave up the world's greatest throne. He spent a month each summer at the *Hôtel du Palais* where he enjoyed perhaps the best of his salad days.

The municipality of Biarritz will do everything possible to prevent this massive red brick building on one side of the Grande Plage from going the way of other grand hotels along the coast. It has preserved into these egalitarian times the all-pervading luxury of these establishments before the great depression, raised to a higher power by such refinements as period furniture in private suites.

Although what we see today is the result of a reconstruction and extension following a fire in 1908, this is one Palace Hotel with a right to the title. For it was built for an Empress. The *Villa Eugénie* was Napoleon III's gift to his Spanish consort, who had spent childhood summers at what was then a tiny Basque fishing hamlet. A short walk round Biarritz is enough to remind anyone who has forgotten all the political manœuvring which went on here during the 1860s that the gay 'twenties were merely the golden sunset of a resort which knew its high noon under the Second Empire.

There are reasons why Napoleon III continues to be badly judged in France, more than a century after the disaster of 1870. But it can be inferred from the attention he receives on the radio, and in all those popular history magazines the French so love, that there is a great nostalgia for his age, notwithstanding the vulgarities of the railway speculators and parvenus who dominated it. When we consider that he presided over France's industrial revolution, we can only wonder that the inevitable errors of taste were committed with so much elegance.

And whatever the rest of the country may think, he and the Empress retain their popularity in the south-west. Theirs was the only period in French history when the head of state, *le pouvoir* to use De Gaulle's impersonal term, resided for long periods in the area covered by this book. For although this region gave France the best king she ever had, to reach the throne Henry IV was obliged not only to accept the Mass, but to leave forever the lands north of the Pyrenees which had cradled and sustained him.

Napoleon III's terrible uncle only came here once, and briefly, in 1808, to humiliate and force into abdication the Spanish royal family whom he had summoned to Bayonne (Hitler was less successful in the interview he had with a later, tougher ruler of Spain at Hendaye in 1940). The impatient little Bonaparte travelled swiftly, as always. Contemporary engravings show his coach crossing the Landes, and being greeted by the outlandish inhabitants on the stilts which enabled them to move over what was then bare, unhealthy marsh.

But the nephew bought an estate in the very heart of the Landes, and by his example in planting pines played a leading part in making it one of the richest—and healthiest—corners of the country. This estate lay astride the new railway line from Paris and Bordeaux, and the branches which fanned out from this, and from the other main line to Toulouse, brought good communications for the first time to a region which even away from the steep mountains had stagnated in the mud of its thick clay soils. The favourite form of nineteenth-century holiday was the health cure, and no area was better endowed with mineral springs. So now that every man could take the train to take the waters, the spas multiplied: one even took the name of *Eugénie-les-Bains*.

The line was extended from Bayonne to the Spanish frontier in 1860, but the Empress of the Railway Age herself preferred that it should not pass directly through her beloved resort. A branch line of a couple of miles had therefore to be constructed later, culminating in a curious two-level station which claims to be inspired by '*l'architecture basque et celle du Nord de l'Espagne*'. In fact it is the town's most exotic building except for the Orthodox church, which at Biarritz as at Nice reminds us how before 1914 France was every Russian's second homeland.

The junction where this branch meets the main line is at La Négresse, beside which the lake of Mouriscot offers between its shady banks the water skiing impossible in the rollers of the Bay of Biscay. But those very rollers have made Biarritz the surfing capital of Europe, since the sport was introduced in the early 'sixties by the daughter of our then Ambassador to Paris, Sir Gladwyn Jebb, and her young French husband.

The transition between worldly resort and timeless Basque countryside represented by La Négresse is fulfilled even more charmingly behind St-Jean-de-Luz by Chantaco, a garden suburb on the grand scale set between golf-courses on either side of the Nivelle. And then in both cases one is back in the hinterland, the *pays basque* without folksy artificiality. In clearings of the forest of St-Pée, within a five-mile radius of both St-Jean-de-Luz and Biarritz, I have spent entire days without seeing a tourist.

But the villages are anxious to look their best to those visitors who can drag themselves away from the coast. The nearest to Biarritz is the utterly delightful Arcangues. A study in red and white against a bosky background, it is preserved of a piece by the Marquis d'Arcangues, who for many years was *maire* of the neighbouring resort. It has a thirteenth-century church.

The concept of a village deliberately modelled by a landowner, however, is by no means in the Basque tradition. This is better represented by Ascain, a rather larger place at the same distance behind St-Jean-de-Luz. This has a Basque pelota *fronton*, a Basque galleried church, and a large number of those spacious half-timbered Basque farmhouses which are at their sprucest yet most archetypal in Labourd.

There are several hotels, built in the same style. You can eat well at Ascain. You may even find inspiration, as did Pierre Loti at the *Hôtel de la Rhune*. There he wrote his Basque novel *Ramuntcho*, before he had acquired a Basque home of his own at Hendaye.

Perhaps he had fallen under the spell of La Rhune, the 3,000 foot mountain almost on the frontier, where once there gathered the witches of Labourd. It can be reached either on foot from Ascain, or during the season on a ratchet railway from the Col de St-Ignace two miles to the south.

Further inland the villages of Sare, Ainhoa and Espelette have the same essential *labourdin* qualities as Ascain, displayed with less self-consciousness and a greater abundance of flowers. Lying only a few miles north of the deserted but easily-crossed frontier, they have a long history of smuggling. They are small. The centres of population in interior Labourd lie behind Biarritz in the middle valley of the Nive, which joins the Adour at Bayonne.

Lowest of these downstream is Ustaritz, traditional capital of Labourd. Here until the Revolution the little province's *maires* met in an assembly called the Bilçar. The nobility was not represented; and in 1789 it was the nobles of Labourd who demanded a share in government with the Third Estate!

Today it has a seminary which tightens the long alliance between the Basque language and the Church. Twenty years ago this was chosen by the Catholic University of Toulouse as the seat of its summer course. This has been so successful that it now has a functional white residential and study centre of its own, a little way outside the town.

Study is hardly the right word. Were it not for its Protestant overtones I would choose rather *colloque* to describe the friendly discussions and debates, led by leading intellectuals from French

Catholicism. These include philosophers, scientists, literary critics, writers, politicians and artists, besides leading clergy. A beloved French agnostic once declared to me with pride that though the Church's bureaucracy might come from Italy, and its financial support from America, its brains were indisputably from France. At Ustaritz you can meet these brains in the flesh, while at the same time you learn French and explore the *pays basque*.

There are pretty little hamlets down narrow lanes off the main road on to Cambo-les-Bains. One such hamlet is Larressore, where since the early nineteenth century the Aincient family, former makers of distaffs, have turned their skill to developing the *makhila*, a supposedly 'typically Basque' weapon-cum-walking-stick in which they have a near-monopoly.

A mile before Cambo stands Arnaga, the *villa basque* to beat all *villas basques*. It was built by the playwright Edmond Rostand, famous for *Cyrano de Bergerac* and for *L'Aiglon*, based on the life of Napoleon's only son, the Duke of Reichstadt. The part was one of the triumphs of Sarah Bernhardt, and souvenirs of her and of other theatrical and literary figures of the early years of the century crowd the panelled or lacquered salons of this suitably theatrical dwelling. The lovely gardens, like the house, can be visited.

It is the gardens of its villas that one remembers of Cambo, very much a *ville fleurie*. But it is the furthest outpost of the residential coast. Beyond lie the last *labourdin* villages, wholly Basque. Hasparren, a name meaning 'within the oaks', is connected directly with Bayonne by an unlikely but inspiring crest-road called the *route impériale des cimes*, built for strategic reasons by Napoleon I. It runs high above the heath or *lande* known as the Bois de Hasparren from the days when it really was a dense oak forest. The tannin from the oaks gave the town first a tanning, and then a footwear industry, which still survives. It is a great pelota centre.

The *pays basque* has many of these heaths, representing former woodland, especially hereabouts where Labourd has no other natural frontier with Basse-Navarre. Such a natural frontier might have been fixed at the Pas de Roland, a man-made tunnel in a rock where the Nive, upstream from Cambo, has narrowed to a gorge. Roland, to whom here as in so many places in the Pyrenees are attributed superhuman achievements, would then have been in the Navarre to which his story belongs.

But instead the boundary curves south to give Labourd Louhossoa, where once I spent a happy week camping at a former hunting-lodge of the Counts of Macaye. It was the pleasantest camp-site I have ever known. The great square white house was open for us to read, play indoor games, or chat with the warden and his wife, a civilized couple retired from Paris who seemed to have taken on the job as a labour of love. But there were only three other tents or caravans besides my own, and perhaps it is no surprise that it has been transformed into a *colonie de vacances*.

Even if the children who stay there are not as lucky as I was, in being able to watch the cyclists of the Tour de France tear down Louhossoa's main street, they will have a wonderful time in the meadows and forests—for not all these have degenerated into heaths. The countryside of Labourd and of Basse-Navarre is the English countryside as it appeared to us as children: greener and more luxuriant, yet milder and drier, than it really is. The characters of Beatrix Potter and Kenneth Grahame would surely adapt themselves with as much enthusiasm as their animal prototypes to these clear little streams and steep little hills and tamed yet tangled woods.

2. BAYONNE

Bayonne is not in fact Basque, although a lot of Basques live there, and although even today one crosses the 'linguistic frontier' immediately on leaving it for the south. For although the port of the *pays basque*, it is also the port of Béarn, Bigorre, the Landes, and the wide slice of Gascony drained by the Adour.

The Adour has been at once Bayonne's cross and her salvation. Though it provided the only safe anchorage of any size between Bordeaux and Pasajes, its dramatic meeting with the Atlantic rollers set up violent sandbank-forming currents. The low, sandy

1. The inner harbour of St-Jean-de-Luz, with its perfect, protected bay beyond

2. The Nive near Cambo

3. 'Discoidal' Basque tombs of mysterious origin

nature of the country to the north made it all too easy for the river, once blocked, to forge itself a new course. At different periods in historical times it emptied itself into the sea at Capbreton, and as far north as Vieux-Boucau (*boucau* being the Gascon for mouth). The reopening of its present estuary in 1578 was artificial, being one of the better legacies of the Charles IX who presided over the Massacre of St-Bartholomew.

Rivers provide Bayonne's framework. The single bridge over the Adour can be a worse bottle-neck than the frontier itself for the streams of summer travellers to Spain. When they have at last negotiated it they must at once turn right to cross another over the tributary Nive. Only then are they in the main part of the city, after briefly crossing its two outlying *faubourgs*. But thanks to the Adour, even they get an impression of civilized leisure as they crawl nose to tail between the calm, shady quays and the arcades at whose terrace cafés *habitués* enjoy, spoonful by spoonful, the hot chocolate in which Bayonne has specialized for three centuries.

Those arcades, like other buildings facing the river, belong to the prosperous period in the eighteenth century when the profits from West Indian trade were supplemented by the prizes brought into port by the *corsaires*, those licensed pirates who operated with such success during the frequent wars against England. But for two centuries before that the enemy had been Hapsburg Spain. Then Bayonne had been a key garrison town. Then the metal workers who armed the garrison devised that cunning weapon which married the terror of the sword to the power of gunpowder: the bayonnette. And away from the river Vauban's ramparts still guard the Porte d'Espagne.

But they were raised when the Spanish menace was already past. The only army which has laid siege before them was that of Wellington in 1813 and 1814. After the battle of Vitoria he successfully forced the Bidassoa and the Nivelle. Inland his campaign was successful all the way to Toulouse. But the Adour remained *non polluta*, as Bayonne's motto reads. Relations between garrison and besiegers were sufficiently good to enable the British

c   *33*

officers to arrange the purchase of various luxuries in the town. But they did not prevent heavy casualties when the French made an unexpected sortie on 14th April 1814. The British fallen lie in two cemeteries a mile up the Bordeaux road.

There was a time when the English were overlords and allies: from Henry of Plantagenet's marriage to Eleanor of Aquitaine in 1152, until in 1451 Bayonne surrendered to Joan of Arc's companion in arms, Dunois, after one of those miraculous signs from Heaven which distinguished the French victories at the close of the Hundred Years War. In its earlier stages Providence was more impartial, and the great Constable of France, Du Guesclin, was imprisoned in the Château Vieux until his ransom arrived.

The monument to that earlier age of prosperity is the Cathedral of Ste-Marie, which with its adjoining cloister belongs essentially to the thirteenth century. It is in northern Gothic, though I always find its interior unexpectedly dark in view of the large windows it owes to that style. This may be because these are filled with fine examples of Renaissance stained glass. Several keystones of the vaulted roof bear English leopards. Those with *fleurs-de-lis* were added after 1451.

Bayonne has two famous and quite different museums. They lie not in its centre, in the busy narrow streets round the cathedral, or the squares and quays on to which these lead, but in the quarter between the Nive and the Adour which we crossed on our way there.

The Musée Bonnat, though a private collection left by the artist Léon Bonnat to his native town, is finer than any Musée des Beaux-Arts in our region. His long life from 1833 to 1922 covered the best years the amateur collector has ever known; and his taste, supported by the fortune he earned as a fashionable portrait painter, was sure. Michelangelo, Leonardo da Vinci, Rubens, Rembrandt, Poussin, Tiepolo, Goya are only the greatest of the names represented. And there are Egyptian statuettes, Tanagra terracottas, and the fourth most important collection of drawings in Europe, besides a room filled with portraits and religious works by Bonnat himself.

The other museum occupies a sixteenth-century house in front of the Nive. Its full title is the *Musée Basque et de la Tradition Bayonnaise*. For the *tradition bayonnaise* is Gascon. Until 1451 Gascon was the town's official language; and as late as 1680 Madame d'Aulnoy found that the upper classes there spoke nothing else.

But the Gascons have been generous enough here to give first place to the Basques, who have no comparable museum in either their French or their Spanish homelands. A roll of honour names the Spanish Basques who have risen to places of importance in Latin America. Costumes and souvenirs recall those dreary Carlist Wars which so divided the Spanish Basques during the last century.

It is the *pays basque* of this side of the Bidassoa, however, which by rights is mainly represented. There are wonderful examples of those discoidal (circular-topped) tombs such as are found in churchyards all over Labourd. Although some date from as late as the nineteenth century, Spanish museums have examples inscribed with characters in the extinct Iberian alphabet, proving them to be pre-Christian in origin. It has been suggested that they may be an anthropomorphic development of the Neolithic menhir.

Other pre-Christian practices survived into the seventeenth century. A horrific series of primitive paintings illustrate the perfectly genuine confessions of witchcraft made before the ecclesiastical court in Labourd. They show witches flying, witches' Sabbaths, witches' orgies, and so on.

There is an entire Basque farmhouse, complete with tools and furniture. There is a museum within a museum celebrating the sport of pelota: its development, its instruments, and some of the champion *pelotari*. Case after case shows the costumes worn by the Basque dancers. One would have to spend a long time in Soule to get as clear an idea of the *souletin* dances as one has after half an hour in the gallery here devoted to them.

It is no reflection on the skill with which it is arranged to say that there is something pleasingly amateurish about the Musée

Basque. One feels that the inscription in Basque above the entrance means what it says:

Hemen sartzen dena
Bere etchean da.

He who comes in here is in his own home.

There is indeed a home here for everyone who has contributed in any way to the *pays basque* or to the *tradition bayonnaise*. Here meets the *Confrérie du Jambon de Bayonne*, the association formed to protect the quality and extend the markets of the famous Bayonne hams.

One small room is filled with documents in a strange tongue which proves to be not Basque, but Hebrew. For in the sixteenth century many families of Portuguese and Spanish Jews established themselves in the *faubourg* of Saint-Esprit, on the other side of the Adour. Like those who went to North Africa, Constantinople or Amsterdam, and like those too who stayed at home to practise their religion in secret, their community had a high capacity for survival. In 1753 Gascony's greatest Intendant, d'Etigny, issued regulations for the 'Nation Portugaise Juive et Espagnole établie au Bourg St-Esprit près Bayonne'. And I have an English friend in Biarritz named Mme Gomez, whose husband proudly traces his ancestry back to those fugitives from the Inquisition.

3. BASSE-NAVARRE

Basse-Navarre is divided from Labourd by the wide heaths or *landes* at which we halted beyond Hasparren and Louhossoa. From Soule it is separated by a series of hills rising from one thousand all the way to five thousand feet. Even without these geographical obstacles, history would have split the French Basques into three distinct provinces. For Basse-Navarre was exactly what it says: lower Navarre, the province beyond the Pyrenees of the little Christian Spanish state which grew up around Pamplona.

Pamplona was in those days a Basque-speaking town, and Navarre might easily have become the political expression of the whole Basque nation. But in 1200 the last king of her native dynasty, though known as Sancho the Strong, lost the coastal Basque provinces of Vizcaya and Guipúzcoa to Castile. And two centuries later the landlocked kingdom was joined in personal union with two other Pyrenean states: Béarn and Foix.

After Castile and Aragon had united, and together conquered Granada, it was therefore a comparatively simple matter for Ferdinand of Aragon to complete the reunion of Spain by bringing his army against Navarre in 1512. Catherine of Foix and her husband Jean d'Albret were obliged to flee to those parts of their dominions which lay north of the Pyrenees. But in marrying they had brought about quite a little reunion of their own: their joint possessions covered almost half our region. So with the help of France they successfully retained most of the *sexta merindad* of their kingdom, Basse-Navarre. Its occupation made their claim to the crown of Navarre more than an empty title.

When their great-grandson Henry of Navarre ascended the French throne, this title was inherited by the kings of France. Until the Revolution the province remained a distinct entity. But it was only after the Spaniards at last evacuated St-Jean-Pied-de-Port at the Peace of the Pyrenees in 1659, that the States or assembly of Basse-Navarre was able to meet in its rightful *Maison des Etats*.

This little fortified town at the foot of Roncevaux seems always to have more than its fifteen hundred inhabitants. For it remains the natural market for the surrounding valleys, just as during the Middle Ages it was the natural gathering point for pilgrims preparing to cross the Pyrenees on their journey to Santiago de Compostela.

There were pirates in the Bay of Biscay in those days, and the coastal road was difficult (it still is). Before the plantation of the pines the Landes were marshy, again deflecting travellers inland. But if they went too far towards the interior they faced the high Pyrenees. Seeking the *juste milieu*, therefore, three of the four principal *routes de St-Jacques* united at Ostabat in Basse-Navarre, and came on to St-Jean-Pied-de-Port together.

The fifteenth-century walls of the oldest part of the town, of which a fortified church forms part, are much as the pilgrims saw them. And the narrow streets, straddling across the Nive on two mossy old bridges, must be quieter than when they offered food and lodging to the devout from all Europe. The centre of animation, as the French say, is now the square outside the walls, where the main road crosses a more modern bridge downstream. Here are some justly famous restaurants. There is an added flavour to a trout consumed overlooking the swift river where it was recently caught.

That river divides here. The Nive proper goes south-east to its source just across the frontier, on the edge of the great forest of Iraty. This also stretches on both sides of that imaginary line, and is now under joint Franco-Spanish exploitation. It is best reached by the D18 from St-Jean-le-Vieux, a village three miles east of St-Jean-Pied-de-Port, whose church has a Romanesque doorway.

The main road to the frontier, the famous road followed by Charlemagne in 778, follows the Petite Nive, which is born in the very pass of Roncevaux. For some miles the stream actually forms the frontier. Here occasional foot-bridges lead to houses on the Spanish side. These are *ventas*, shops-cum-bars stocking all those goods and drinks which are cheaper in Spain. Nothing prevents the tourist crossing the foot-bridge and making his purchases, but he does so at his own risk. For French customs do not operate only at the actual frontier. Many miles in the interior a polite hand raised at the side of the road, or a uniformed motor-cyclist purposefully overtaking, signal one of those spot checks which are infinitely more thorough than that given by the nonchalantly smiling *douanier* who only seemed interested in our green insurance card.

There is yet another Nive, named after its isolated valley the Nive des Aldudes. This only joins the other two Nives seven miles downstream from St-Jean-Pied-de-Port. It is more easily reached through Irouléguy, where the best wine of the *pays basque* is grown, and the reposeful little town of St-Etienne-de-Baïgorry, with one of the few Basque castles, of the sixteenth century.

But the full measure of repose lies upstream from St-Etienne. I have described in another book how I once proceeded beyond the last hamlet of les Aldudes, Urepel, to the very frontier, and had a Spanish lunch at the first of the *ventas* I ever encountered. But that *venta* marked the end of the road. Here in les Aldudes, as at the head of so many valleys on both sides as we proceed east, we can each find our personal 'peace of the Pyrenees'.

Not that Basse-Navarre is anywhere exactly noisy. Simply because the hills are higher than in Labourd, the villages in their green basins, such as Iholdy, twelve miles north of St-Jean-Pied-de-Port, each belong to their own little world. The *fronton* for pelota is universal throughout the *pays basque*, but other features differ from those of Labourd. Few houses have any half-timbering, and their well-cut cornerstones give them a firmer, less 'pretty pretty' appearance. Churchyards have not only the 'discoidal' tomb, but often one formed by a cross atop a wavy base, peculiar to Basse-Navarre. (This fondness for flowing lines reappears in the solid commas which are a frequent motif in Basque decoration, four of which joined together at their points constitute the 'Basque cross', a variety of swastika of uncertain significance.)

On a side road to Hasparren lie our first Pyrenean grottoes: the caves of Oxocelhaya and Isturits. Although visited together, they are quite different in interest. The first are as nature made them, and their stalagmites and stalactites give 'that sinister race of guides who lurk in caverns' as they have been wittily described, the opportunity to point out incongruous likenesses to animals, churches, historical personalities, and so on.

The second, however, were inhabited by men of the Old Stone Age during five hundred centuries. They have left behind rock carvings not only of the vanished reindeer, but of *equus celticus*, a pony whose descendants, the half-wild *pottoka* as the Basques call them, still graze on the *landes* of Labourd.

In the north Basse-Navarre all but reaches the Adour, in a Basque salient around Bardos and Guiche. This is squeezed between two villages of Gascon tradition: Labastide-Clairence built in 1314 on a regular plan it still preserves; and Bidache, with a magnificently-sited castle to which the dearest of all Henry IV's mistresses, la belle Corisande, gave a Renaissance face-lift. The tributary which enters the Adour after flowing round this salient is itself proof of the conflict of cultures. For it bears the alternative names of Joyeuse and Aran, the second of which in Basque means a valley.

There is another Joyeuse in Basse-Navarre. It rises north of St-Jean-Pied-de-Port, and joins the Bidouze, which has risen to the east, just beyond St-Palais. This, the second most important place in the province, was the capital of French Navarre while St-Jean-Pied-de-Port was still occupied by Spain, and was the seat of its high court. Today it is a great centre of Basque folklore, especially of Basque wrestling, although it lies on the very edge of the *pays basque*.

The frontier lies just to the north of the D11 through St-Palais. The villages along that road, many with recognizably Basque names like Garris or Domezain, are *euskara* in speech and sentiments. The physiognomy of their wiry, high-cheeked, long-nosed inhabitants is the same as those of distant Alava and Vizcaya. But the scattering of hamlets immediately to the north belongs as unequivocally to Béarn.

4. SOULE

The traveller who instead of going north from St-Palais continues east along the D11 can be forgiven if he thinks that he too has entered Béarn. And anyone who from St-Jean-Pied-de-Port follows the N618—that *route des Pyrénées* which all the way to the Mediterranean keeps as near the crest as a main road can—may well believe that in passing the low but dramatic Col d'Osquich he has left the *pays basque* behind. For here are no white walls under red tiles. The solid stone houses with their steeply pitched slate roofs are almost a *béarnais* trade-mark.

Yet the three little gables, each with its bell, which rise above many of the churches, symbolizing the Holy Trinity, must belong to some distinct sub-culture. And the churchyards share the same serene quality as those of Labourd and Basse-Navarre, though their tombs are more likely to take the form of rectangles than of circles or wavy crosses. *Orhoit hilceaz*: remember death.

It requires no inscription, however, to tell us that villages with names which end as do Undurein or Berrogain are Basque in origin, or that a town called Mauléon-Soule must be the capital of a *pays* of that name. Indeed Soule, just because it is so isolated, has shown a special persistence in preserving its highly individual Basque culture. The *souletin* dialect has many characteristics of its own; and not all the words I had learned in Guipúzcoa could be understood there—though the very fact that I tried to use them was warmly appreciated. But in the villages around Mauléon, and beyond Mauléon all the way up the Saison valley, it is in regular daily use; whereas in the Spanish valleys of Salazar and Roncal immediately south of the mountains, it has unhappily died out.*

It is less frequently heard in the busy little town itself, where *espadrilles* are manufactured beneath the ruins of a fifteenth-century castle. But then Mauléon has always been receptive to outside influences. The palace of Bishop Maytie of Oloron, at the corner where the *route des Pyrénées* reaches the town centre, is the only substantial example of Renaissance architecture in the entire *pays basque*.

The 'trinity-gabled' churches of Gotein and Sauguis can be seen while covering the eight miles from Mauléon up to Tardets, the centre of Haute-Soule. The dancers from here and from Licq-Atherey perform the Mascarade, an extraordinary medieval survival in which all the performers are either Reds (*Goriak*) or Blacks (*Beltzeia*). The former include the *cherrero* or outrider, the *gathia* or cat, the *kukullerak* or pages, the *marechalak* or marshals, and the *Jaun* and *Andéria* or Gentleman and Lady.

---

* I discuss this in *The Spanish Pyrenees* (Faber and Faber 1966), page 90, 'The Dying Tongue'.

Most famous of the Reds, however, is the *zamalzain*, a centaur-like figure wearing a skirted wickerwork framework. He is supposed to represent the Lord of the village. In fact, however, he is a thinly-disguised phallic virility symbol, like the hobby-horse of English morris dancing he so closely resembles. And significantly the Blacks number not only the *tchorotchak* or knife-grinders, who act as a choir; the *bouhamiak* or gipsies, possibly a folk-memory of the 'untouchable' *cagots*; and the *kauterak* or tinkers, to whom falls the role of clowns; but also the *kestouak* or horse-castrators, who dog the steps of the bucking *zamalzain*.

Soule's unique *Pastorales* give a similar opportunity for division into two sides of 'goods' and 'bads'. With such titles as *Charlemagne*, *Joan of Arc*, *Napoleon*, or *The Great War*, they give plenty of scope to the local writers and actors, and last literally all day—on average about nine hours.

The conventions of the medieval theatre here survive intact: separate entrances for the 'goods' and the 'bads', representational rather than realistic 'battles' and 'deaths', a naïve anachronism in costumes, and frequent intervals for dancing or clowning. Spectacles of such size and duration cannot be everyday events. Nowadays the whole of Haute-Soule has to combine its talents to mount one every few years.

The most recent, in 1966, was given at Trois-Villes, a couple of miles below Tardets (the home of its author, M. Etchahoun), in the beautiful grounds of Elissabea. This country house was built in 1653 on the plans of Mansart himself, by the Comte de Trois-Villes, better known as Tréville to readers of Dumas père.

The two other musketeers were also from only a few miles away, though just outside Soule. For Porthos lived at Lanne, while Aramis was lay abbot of Aramitz in the *béarnais* valley of Barétous, into which the N618 descends as soon as it has climbed from Tardets up to Montory.

Also in Barétous lies Arette, which has built itself 'the nearest winter sports resort to the Basque Coast'. Indeed the ski-station very nearly is within the *pays basque*, as its name 'Arette-Pierre St-Martin' indicates. For the Pierre St-Martin marks where

Barétous and Soule meet Spain, and has been the site each 13th July since 1375 of the ceremonial payment of three tribute cattle from the valley of Barétous to the valley of Roncal in Navarre.

Both the stone, and a nearby cave which has provided speleologists with delight and disaster, can also be reached from Ste-Engrâce, at the head of one of the two valleys into which the Saison divides five miles above Tardets. It is the more interesting of the two, though I must say that I enjoyed them both. This was in large part because after walking to Ste-Engrâce I was lucky enough to be given a lift down its valley, and all the way up the other one to Larrau, by a *souletin* delivering wine. To my surprise every third house seemed to be a *bistro*, though none were advertised as such. We had a drink at every one of them, while my companion proudly got me to bring out my few words of Basque.

This was the only part of the *pays basque* to have glaciers during the Ice Age. Even these were not very powerful, and in three places where their broad, smooth glacial valleys ended, the melted waters cut themselves deep, trench-like passages such as were produced in similar conditions all over the Spanish Pyrenees. These three are the Crevasses d'Holçarte, up a subsidiary valley on the way to Larrau, and the Gorges d'Uzarre and the deservedly famous Gorges de Kakouetta running into the valley below Ste-Engrâce.

The Gorges of Kakouetta must be visited late in the summer when the waters are low. They were only discovered at the turn of the century in the course of surveys for a projected transpyrenean railway. But the two main valleys have been well-trodden since time immemorial. It is only modern communications, bringing Mauléon within half an hour's drive, and making it easier to reach Pamplona the long—and legal—way round, that have turned Larrau and Ste-Engrâce into 'ends of the world'.

The contrast with yesteryear was well illustrated when, after looking round Larrau, I was kindly given a lift back to Tardets by a man in his thirties, dressed in leisure clothes that would not have looked out of place at St-Tropez. He had been spending a day fishing in the valley of his birth, and on the back seat of his

Citroën DS sat his two old aunts, on their way to stay with his mother. They were as darkly-dressed and crone-like as their contemporaries in the hamlets at the head of the Spanish valleys, Uztárroz or Izalzu, which Larrau so resembles. With nostalgia they recalled their childhood: 'Yes, it was a great day when a party of Spaniards used to arrive from over the mountains.'

The great age of these now deserted routes was centuries earlier, when the destination of their traffic lay in the other direction. For here too passed pilgrims leaning on the staff of St. James; and a mile beyond the village of Ste-Engrâce stands a lonely eleventh-century Romanesque basilica, its thick walls and buttresses fortifying it surely as much against the cold as against any enemy. It has a fine carved doorway and capitals, and an unexpected fourteenth-century choir-screen.

Throughout the Spanish Pyrenees Romanesque is not merely the first, but the only style of architecture. For after their moment of glory, early in the Reconquest, life ebbed away from them. The *pays basque* has continued to enjoy a modest prosperity, but its own earliest monuments have a similar origin. Until about A.D. 1000 it must have been a wild, uncivilized region. Then, with the increasing strength and stability of the kingdom of Navarre, came the growth of the *route de St-Jacques*, and the provision during the eleventh and twelfth centuries of chapels and hospices for those who followed it.

Most moving of these in its simplicity and isolation is the Hôpital-St-Blaise, eight miles east of Mauléon. This twelfth-century construction consists of a Greek cross round a central cupola, resting on a short octagonal tower. Though sometimes described as *mudéjar*, built that is by Arabs under Christian rule, I feel it more likely that returning crusaders provided its inspiration, for Arabs had receded a long way from this quiet Catholic sanctuary by the twelfth century. It lies in fact just halfway between Roncevaux with which legend erroneously associates them, and the Somport across which they had briefly raided four hundred years before.

L'Hôpital-St-Blaise marks the very limit of Soule. But the

seventy-odd inhabitants of the tiny hamlet are not quite the last speakers of Basque. A single household also preserves the ancient tongue although it lives a few hundred yards further on, over the border in Béarn.

Chapter 2

BÉARN

I. ALONG THE GAVES

The river Saison, whose valley is Soule, is also known as the Gave de Mauléon. *Gave* was simply a local word meaning river, just as the local word near Luchon was *neste*, and the local word in the valley of Arán was *artiga*. But although one speaks of the Neste d'Oueil or the Artiga de Lín, it is only in Comminges or Arán that one might dream of speaking in a general way of *nestes* or *artigas*. *Gave*, on the other hand, has found its way into the *Petit Larousse*, whose customarily concise and satisfactory definition runs: 'Terme générique sous lequel on désigne, dans le Béarn et la Bigorre, les torrents issus des Pyrénées centrales.'

Though the area concerned is limited, it had as we shall see considerable economic and political importance. And just because it is circumscribed, it has enabled a local word for river in general to become a general word for a particular sort of river. 'Like a Pyrenean *gave*': and at once we have a vision of a shallow, swiftly-running stream, foaming white over smoothly-worn stones where it is not crystal clear, and flowing between lush green water-meadows backed by fir forest.

This is an accurate enough description of their upper course. But the two principal *gaves* of Béarn, which take their names from the towns of Oloron and Pau, are a good deal more than torrents once they have left the mountains.

Their valleys were the very axis of the little viscounty which grew up in this southernmost corner of the Duchy of Gascony. Taking its name from Beneharnum, the Roman name for Lescar, in its ninth-century beginnings it consisted simply of the diocese of Lescar on the Gave de Pau. Then early in the eleventh century the adjoining Viscounty of Oloron on the parallel Gave was added by marriage, and wars with the Viscounts of Dax enabled the strengthened state to acquire almost all the promontory of land between them.

From this restricted but compact base, by judicious marriages and politic alliances, the rulers of Béarn gradually extended their sway over *pays* after *pays* whose melodious names convey a vision of their scenery even before we have visited them. Late in the eleventh century the Montanérès: in the twelfth the Gabardan: in the thirteenth Marsan, Foix, and the co-princedom of Andorra: in the fourteenth the Nebouzan, the sud-Albigeois, and Lautrec: in the fifteenth Soule, Navarre, and Albret. Between them these cover half our region, and at the beginning of the sixteenth century they appeared like a Pyrenean buffer state between France and Spain.

The whole process had been a *tour de force* making use of particular historical circumstances. Béarn was able to achieve independence because the Dukes of Gascony in 1058 became Dukes of Aquitaine, moving their seat of power to Poitiers far in the north, and bequeathing their title a century later to the Eleanor of Aquitaine who married Henry II of England. The Viscounts of Béarn, meanwhile, completed the break with Gascony by a close association with the growing kingdom of Aragon south of the Pyrenees. One of them helped to capture Saragossa in 1118. Another was killed in 1229 leading the Aragonese landing in Mallorca.

They then began a long and profitable balancing act between their three powerful but distant neighbours of London, Paris and Barcelona. Sometimes this meant unfortunate involvements. The Béarnais, though untouched by the Cathare heresy, were defeated along with the Aragonese by Simon de Montfort at Muret in 1213. They were at the side of Henry III of England when St. Louis crushed him at Taillebourg in 1242.

More frequently, however, it meant neutrality, and the commercial fruits of neutrality. While Languedoc writhed under the terrible Albigensian Crusade, transpyrenean traffic was diverted through Béarn over the Somport. And although the Counts of Foix were sometimes obliged, as French vassals, to assist the French crown, they took no sides in their other capacity as Viscounts of Béarn. So while the Hundred Years War raged in Gascony and Guienne, trade which normally flowed from Atlantic to Mediterranean along the Garonne was diverted along the Gaves.

We shall find constant reminders of Béarn's history as we explore these valleys and the long promontory of land between them. The extremely busy road from Bayonne to Pau runs beside the Gave de Pau from Peyrehorade, just below its junction with the Gave d'Oloron. The importance of the site is marked by the fourteenth-century castle of Montréal, with its four square towers, beside the river, and the ruins of the later château of Aspremont on the hill above.

Three miles downstream on the opposite bank stands Hastingues, founded in the thirteenth century by the English Sénéchal John of Hastings to protect this same important waterway. His gateway still stands. All over the south-west French and English alike were planting these *bastides*,* partly to populate empty regions, and partly for defence against each other. Significantly, we shall find none of them once we enter neutral Béarn.

But before doing so, we must visit two abbeys. That of Arthous, with a Romanesque church in process of restoration, is on a narrow country road equidistant between Hastingues and Peyrehorade. Sorde l'Abbaye is even more of an oasis of quiet. For it lies at the very tip of the promontory, a tip which the Béarnais never succeeded in occupying, and it overlooks a wide weir across the Gave d'Oloron. If offers three distinct levels of interest.

Going backwards in time, the first are the remains of the

---

* For a fuller discussion of the *bastides*, see pages 193-4 of *Three Rivers of France* by Freda White (Faber and Faber).

4. The farms of Béarn have steeply pitched slate roofs

5. Basque cross in Soule

6. Hastingues, where the Gave flows slower and broad, still preserves the name of its thirteenth-century English founder

7. The arcade frames a street in Bidache, where Gascony meets the Pays Basque

8. Salies-de-Béarn:
houses of the
parts-prenant or
salt shareholders

seventeenth- and eighteenth-century monastic buildings. Most memorable of these is a subterranean gallery giving on to the weir, a sort of delightful 'cloister with a view'.

Then comes the lofty twelfth- and thirteenth-century church, with a mosaic behind the high altar depicting a hare hunt. Although all the guidebooks assert that this comes from a nearby Roman villa, I was assured on the spot that it dates from the twelfth century, like the church itself. I am inclined to side with the locals, as its style resembles that of the twelfth-century hunting mosaic of Lescar, less than forty miles away up the same valley.

But Sorde has plenty of genuine Roman mosaics, for the abbey was built on the site of a villa, whose central heating system can be made out as we step carefully amongst its excavated foundations. Roman civilization flourished in the lush south-west, outside the Basque country. This and another villa a mile further up the road were within easy distance of all the amenities and hot baths of Dax.

It is surprising that Salies-de-Béarn, eight miles on from Sorde, and a similar distance from each of the *Gaves*, was never exploited by the Romans. Its waters were first put to commercial rather than therapeutic use, and the hams of Béarn, preserved with the salt from the *salies*, were already famous in the Middle Ages. Their export down the Adour was the origin of the *jambons de Bayonne* of today.

The wealth thus created made Salies an important nucleus of the *bourgeoisie* which was Béarn's backbone. The houses of these *parts-prenant* or salt shareholders, grouped to the south of the three bridges over the Saleys river, have more life in their old age than the pleasant but artificial spa which has grown up north of the stream.

The earliest notability to visit Salies for health reasons was Jeanne d'Albret, mother of Henry of Navarre. Generally she lodged at her nearby castle of Bellocq, overlooking the Gave de Pau. But in 1568 she stayed in the town itself, and the Maison Lafont, where her fifteen-year-old son slept, still stands. She was a formidable Protestant, and a huge *temple* of the Reformed Church

D

stands to prove that Béarn was never wholly won back to Catholicism.

The waters used today for the manufacture of salt rather than gynæcological treatments come not from Salies itself, but from Oraas, a village five miles away on the Gave d'Oloron. For several nights I enjoyed there the hospitality of John and Dorothy Gates at their lovely *béarnais* home, whose name, *Houn Salade*, means simply salt fountain (the *h* of *houn* having evolved from an *f*, like the Spanish *hablar*, to talk, from *fablar*).

The Gates's delicious dinners, and their smooth lawns beneath an isolated height called the Pène de Mu, were like a brief resurrection of the English colony round Pau reflected in Dornford Yates. There was an air of the 'twenties, too, in their social life, thanks to which I acquired an insider's view of several of the villages of those glorious middle reaches of the Gave d'Oloron.

Beyond Athos (recalling another of Dumas's musketeers—none of whom was 'Gascon' except in the most general sense) comes Sauveterre-de-Béarn. Here a ruined keep and a thirteenth-century church watch over a wooded cliff above a sharp bend in the *gave*. Into this juts, Avignon-like, the only remaining arch of a fortified bridge, whose legend is told charmingly if naïvely by the paintings under the fortified gateway where the bridge breaks off. Sancie, widow of a twelfth-century viscount of Béarn, was accused of murdering his posthumously-born child; and her brother the King of Navarre ordered her trial by water at this very spot. The pictures show her being thrown into the *gave* with hands and feet bound. It is reassuring to know that she was washed safely ashore, and thus proved innocent of this unlikely crime.

As I have indicated, this is a valley of gracious living. At Laas, five miles on, the park and gardens of a country house and its beautifully-furnished interior have been preserved and opened to the public by the Touring-Club de France. And another five miles on, at Castetnau on the opposite bank, Mrs. Wingfield, the greatest English-speaking authority on this area, is prepared to share her wisdom with guests and tenants who come to stay at her *manoir* and its converted dependencies.

Mrs. Wingfield's knowledge of *béarnais* lore includes that of traditional nature cures. She related how she herself was healed of shingles.

The cure had to be performed between sunset and sunrise, and at a north-south, east-west cross-roads (where two suitably orientated corridors meet would be equally efficacious). The healer can be anyone who has had shingles, and who himself believes in the cure. Mrs. Wingfield herself would therefore qualify. For although the healer ought in theory to carry his patient, it is in fact sufficient for the patient to lean heavily against the healer during the cure.

This consists of the healer criss-crossing the point of inter-section seven times, throwing down his cummerbund, which someone else picks up, and repeating seven times the words 'Je porte'. To this the patient as often replies with the mysterious formula 'Le zona'.

This was first carried out late at night, and again early in the morning. Already by the following afternoon Mrs. Wingfield was much better. A third repetition completed her recovery, officially attested when she was visited by her amazed nurse and doctor.

There is a steep climb to Castetnau, and an equally steep climb across the valley to Navarrenx. One look at its cunningly designed ramparts: recessed gates, round surfaces, and that skilful marriage of a stone shell to deep earthworks which combines strength with elasticity, and the initiated cries 'Vauban'.

But we are in Béarn where, just as they had no bastides, so as early as 1537 they commissioned the Veronese Fabrici Siciliano to design these up-to-date fortifications, the first of their kind in France, almost a century before Vauban was born. In 1563 one of Philip II's spies reported their strength. In 1569 they alone resisted the Catholic invasion of Béarn.

There are one or two nice old houses within the ramparts. One is the home of the Comtesse de Longueil, cousin of the English Queen Mother. An earlier and less proper royal personage, Henry of Navarre, rendered at Navarrenx to Corisande, perhaps the dearest of his loves, 'the greatest homage a lady can obtain from her cavalier. Their night of love took place on the standards pierced with cannon balls, and the blood-stained flags taken at the battle of Coutras by the prince who, for love of her, had just gained a victory.'

Navarrenx proudly calls itself 'capitale du saumon', and holds a world salmon fishing championship each year at Easter and again early in July. But John Gates, who was actually drawn to settle by the Gave d'Oloron by this publicity, told me that his disappointment with the fishing was only equalled by his disgust at the way his discreet attempts to 'keep' the game on his estate were sabotaged in the interests of 'chasse libre', that rallying cry of the *paysan* ever since 1789.

Oloron, from which the *gave* takes its name, stands appropriately where this takes birth at the junction of the two tributary *gaves* of Aspe and Ossau, Pyrenean torrents in Larousse's sense to whose valleys we shall be devoting a separate section. Split by these waters into three, it is a difficult town to drive through. Its full name, Oloron-Ste-Marie, refers either to the town as a whole, or to the district to the left of both *gaves*, grouped around one of the many cathedrals which lost their episcopal status at the Revolution. Built by the Viscount of Béarn who returned from the First Crusade, it has a magnificent Romanesque doorway, whose figures include two Saracens in fetters, and the viscount himself on horseback.

Oloron was an important halt on that *route de St-Jacques* which entered Spain by the Somport. A pilgrimage in the opposite direction, a sad one of refugees from the Spanish Civil War, has made of the ancient quarter of Ste-Croix almost a Spanish colony. For a century there has also been a settlement there of Spanish Protestants. It scrambles up the steep hill between the two tributary streams, around a Romanesque church slightly older, if less perfect, than Ste-Marie, with fine views from its terrace and from the Promenade Bellevue above the Gave d'Aspe.

There are three sizeable towns on the other main *gave* of Béarn. But Pau, from which it takes its name, demands a section to itself; and Lourdes is over the border in Bigorre, where the torrent has its source. So the smallest of the three, Orthez, twenty miles upstream from Peyrehorade, can here be allowed the pre-eminence it once enjoyed.

Though only two monuments survive from the years between 1194 and 1464 when it was the capital of Béarn, both have a significance beyond the intrinsic. The thirteenth-century fortified bridge, reached by a narrow lane from the main road, is intact, though it was the scene of fighting during Wellington's victory at Orthez in 1814. Today it bears almost as little traffic as Sauveterre's stump. But it was the early construction of bridges at Orthez, Sauveterre and Oloron which gave to the *béarnais* merchants their grip on the medieval carrying trade, and hence to the little viscounty its political importance.

That political importance is symbolized by the Tour Moncade above the town, the thirteenth-century keep which alone remains of the viscounts' palace. For it was during the centuries when Orthez was capital that Béarn, as Béarn, knew its moment of glory. The viscounts who later ruled from Pau figure more prominently in general history, but only because they were also kings of Navarre, and close relations by marriage of the French royal family. Their predecessors, it is true, were also Counts of Foix from 1290 onwards, but Béarn was their strength, and Orthez their home. And it was one of their number who made the dream of a truly independent Pyrenean state a triumphant reality for sixty years.

The achievement of Gaston 'Phoebus' was in every sense personal. The very nickname, with its classical overtones, leaps like a flash of Renaissance lightning from the feudal fourteenth century, just as the physique and golden hair which earned it marked him out amongst his contemporaries. Renaissance, too, was the almost Machiavellian manner in which the prince ignored the *For* or constitution of Béarn, and the way in which he cunningly grew rich, leaving his Treasury with the unheard-of sum of 750,000 gold florins. This was largely due to his profitable neutrality: though he could raise an army of 6,000 within forty-eight hours, he preferred to be paid for *not* fighting.

So while the French and English struggled, high court was held at Orthez. Froissart, visiting there in 1388, described the trappings of chivalry which surrounded this one-time vassal of Gascony, who now dealt as an equal with the lord of all Aquitaine: the Black Prince at Bordeaux.

But Renaissance methods a century before their time provoked feudal reactions. The nobility, deprived of influence by Gaston Phoebus, conspired with his only son to poison him. When the plot was discovered the latter was imprisoned in the Tour Moncade. A meeting between father and son led to a violent quarrel, during which the viscount, in a fit of passion, stabbed his offspring to death.

After this tragedy his personal achievement was subject, even more than most personal achievements, to the laws of mortality. Perhaps his realization of this was the reason for his strange will, leaving Béarn to the French crown. He had no right to do this; and the States of Béarn, meeting at Orthez, gave the regency to one of his bastards, and the eventual succession to a cousin.

In certain respects at least he was a child of his own time. Apart from his enjoyment of pageantry, and of chivalric poetry—of which he was himself no mean practitioner in his native *béarnais*—he delighted in bear hunting. It was on one such expedition that he died in 1391, killed not by the bear, but by an apoplexy brought on by his joy at hearing of the death of his enemy Jean d'Armagnac.

Bears roamed wider afield in those days. For his last hunt Gaston Phoebus had only to travel six miles south of Orthez, to L'Hôpital d'Orion, a Gothic version of L'Hôpital-St-Blaise, with the same plan of a Greek cross. Though long neglected, and more than once restored, he would still recognize it.

He would soon find himself lost, however, if he were to leave his old capital and travel on up the *gave*, towards where immense torches never cease to burn high above the valley. They signal the source of the greatest prosperity Béarn has known since his own age.

The Société Nationale des Pétroles d'Aquitaine made the first commercially worthwhile discovery of petrol in France here at Lacq in 1949. Two years later, and five times deeper—further below the ground than the Pyrenean peaks rise above it—came the more important discovery of vast quantities of natural gas. Its effect on this agricultural, thinly populated and economically stagnant countryside was far more dramatic than that of North Sea gas on the already industrialized lands of northern Europe. This clean, welcome fuel is now carried by pipeline all over the south-west. There are even cars and vans which run off it, their engines being fed by long cylinders on their roofs.

Around Lacq itself a whole new series of industries has grown up. There are factories for purifying this hot, high-pressure gas, for extracting sulphur from it, for developing plastics, for the electrolysis of aluminium, and for producing petro-chemicals.

A whole new town, Mourenx-Ville-Nouvelle, has been built in an imaginative functional style to house those who have come to work in them. And provision is made, by carefully-chosen developments in the surrounding countryside, for those who wish to live in more traditional homes. So villages like Monein, with the only important Gothic church in Béarn, are also benefiting from the riches beneath them.

You can visit Mourenx-Ville-Nouvelle. You can also enjoy a free accompanied visit over the plant at Lacq. If you haven't the time you may still think it worth your while to pull up at the unfamiliar-looking petrol station there. *Super* and *Ordinaire* are at the same high, controlled price as anywhere else in France. But it imparts a feeling of belonging to purr onwards towards Pau on *essence du pays*.

2. PAU

One wonders if some geo-political necessity caused the viscounts of Béarn to transfer their capital from Orthez to the castle of Pau in 1464. For it lay only four miles upstream from their earliest capital, the Roman city of Beneharnum down by the *gave*, of which nothing remains since its destruction by a Moslem raid in 841.

As at St-Bertrand-de-Comminges nearly seventy miles east, a new town rose on the hill behind, and retained, like the ghost of its former political importance, an ecclesiastical primacy. The bishops of Lescar presided over the States of Béarn, and their twelfth-century cathedral became a Westminster Abbey or St. George's Chapel after the union with Navarre. Twelve members of the royal family were buried here; and although their tombs were destroyed at the Revolution, ingenious if somewhat grisly excavations have enabled the bones of several to be identified with certainty. There is a moral to be found in this equation of the beautiful and brilliant Marguerite d'Angoulême with poor Yorick.

After giving them the moment of reflection they deserve, the tourist should enjoy the Romanesque capitals, the carved seventeenth-century stalls, and above all the great mosiac in the choir. Dating from the period of the cathedral's construction, it includes a famous representation of a one-legged, dark-skinned archer. As at L'Hôpital-St-Blaise, we wonder if the artist met him on Crusade, or if he wandered up from Spain.

Few cities with less than a six-figure population, and with a relatively short history by European standards, are able to evoke so many different responses as Pau. The visitor who can share in these responses will gain a deeper understanding of a clean, attractive town which may strike him at first as bright but unwelcoming.

This superficial brittleness is identifiable at once by those familiar with Western Germany or Midland England. It is one of the less pleasant by-products of prosperity: a busy unfriendliness associated with overtime, with more money than leisure, and with the immigration of technical and administrative experts without local connexions.

It is the natural gas of Lacq and its dependent industries which have brought these, and the new shops which have risen to serve them. But as they brush past us with their *chariots* full of groceries in the supermarkets, or perilously overtake us on that racing track known as *Route Nationale 117*, it is worth considering how they themselves look at the city they have done so much to alter.

For these *cadres*—the word, meaning literally 'frames', corresponds to our 'executives'—the transfer to Pau has been in every sense an entry into lusher pastures. Not only has it generally meant promotion, but also a move to a slower, softer world. *Le sud-ouest* in France has very similar connotations to those of 'the south-west' in England, except that the French south-west is wider and warmer, with mountains instead of mere moors, with forests instead of woods, and with thousands of geese and ducks as well as fat cattle in the green meadows by the *gaves*. 'Those who have once tasted the *sud-ouest* can never really settle anywhere else' said a wise old English friend who had finally retired from his Paris business to a manor amongst chestnut woods, ten miles south of Pau.

So these outsiders appreciate the quality of life they seem so bent on destroying. And they have arrived with at least one prejudice in common with the natives. This is an overwhelming admiration for the greatest native of all.

He was born in 1553 in the Renaissance château which had grown up around a hunting lodge of the viscounts of Béarn. Although it is considerably restored, and filled with many valuable objects—especially tapestries—which have little direct connexion with the region, the room where Henry IV first saw the light still holds his tortoise-shell cradle. Béarn itself is looked after in a special museum in one of the wings.

The very fact that her greatest son has been claimed by the country as a whole well illustrates the problem of Béarn and of all the French provinces. 'Paris vaut bien une messe,' his alleged quip when he changed his religion to win over the fiercely Catholic capital, has a somewhat bitter sound to *béarnais* ears. For the road to Paris was the road away from home, and the mass thus accepted was to be imposed on his own people only ten years after his assassination in 1610.

The history of Protestantism in Béarn was short but exciting.

Its introduction by Henry's mother, the virago Jeanne d'Albret, led in 1569 to the most savage invasion the province ever suffered. But after the Catholic tide had rolled back Pau became for thirty years a 'petit Génève', as his bride the French princess Margot described it. Like her contemporary Mary Queen of Scots in Holyrood, she was allowed to hear mass privately at the château. But she could do nothing to prevent the arrest of any *béarnais* catholic who dared to attend it. Attendance on the other hand at the *temples*, as the churches were renamed, became compulsory. Ecclesiastical property was taken over and sold, and a Protestant University was established at Orthez.

Calvinism's monopoly in Béarn ended in 1598 with the Edict of Nantes. For the *quid pro quo* of toleration for the Protestants in the rest of France was toleration for the Catholics in Béarn. But it might have remained the religion of most of the population if the Reformed Church of Béarn had not unwisely merged itself with the Reformed Church of France as a whole in 1616. For religion and politics could not in that age be separated. When an excuse presented itself, no local sentiment prevented Henry IV's son, Louis XIII, from making his one and only visit to Pau in 1620, finally to attach Béarn to the throne of France, and to impose Catholicism there as in all his dominions.

From then on the pressure to conform was continuous. Even before the Revocation of the Edict of Nantes in 1685—that blunder of Louis XIV which enriched with Huguenots lands as distant as Prussia, South Africa and Ulster—the number of *temples* in Béarn was down to five. And the only places in Béarn with an unbroken history of organized Protestantism right up to today are Osse in the valley of Aspe and Araujuzon on the Gave d'Oloron. With a thrill I saw an *Hôtel du Temple* on the Rue du Temple at Arthez, only to discover that the temple itself had long since ceased to exist!

In view of these actions of Louis XIII and Louis XIV it can be understood that Béarn's affection was for the memory of Henry of Navarre, rather than for his descendants on the throne of France. The States of Béarn, asked by the Intendant to erect a

statue to Louis XIV at Pau, after long delays grudgingly con-
sented. But it was on foot, instead of being one of those equestrian
Baroque extravaganzas in which the Sun King delighted. And
its inscription was even more down to earth: 'Acy qu'ey l'arréhil
dou nouste gran Henric'.* 'Here is the grandson of our great
Henry.'

It is interesting that the future pretender, Henry V, was so
christened in 1820 because the Bourbons tried to make use of
their great ancestor's popularity when they were restored. In an
effort to trade on that popularity, the Duke of Angoulême tried
to visit Pau as soon as the English took it in 1814. But Wellington,
neutral in French internal affairs even towards the legitimists,
refused him permission, and stopped manifestations in favour of
Louis XVIII.

We shall often hear of 'Our great Henry', and of his exploits in
love and war, as we travel across our region. For the lands which
he inherited long before he became King of France ran from
Basse-Navarre to Foix, and all the way up to Nérac. Indeed,
his spirit presides over the lands north of the Pyrenees much as
his friend Montaigne's presides over the lands further north
described by Freda White in *Three Rivers of France*.

Few men after four hundred years can at once be recognized
under so many names: *Henri Quatre, Henri le Grand, Henri de
Navarre, le Vert-Galant* (in reference to his ability to enjoy
fully his favourite sport into advanced middle age). But perhaps
the most revealing is the one which came most frequently to
the lips of his contemporaries: *le béarnais*.

For not only was he born at Pau: he grew up in the countryside round about. His grandfather's first action on the infant's
arrival was to rub his lips with garlic, and then wet them with
Jurançon, the most famous wine of Béarn. This sweet golden

---

* *Béarnais* remained the official language of the States of Béarn right up to the
Revolution. It is worth noting that these States never sanctioned Louis XIII's
attachment of the viscounty to the crown. When the States General declared France
unified on 4th August 1789, therefore, the leader of the *Béarnais* Third Estate,
Mourot, insisted this must be ratified at Pau. But the States of Béarn defeated the
proposal, and Mourot was obliged to get it approved by 'direct democracy' in public
meetings in the larger towns and villages.

nectar, of high alcoholic content, is cultivated not only in the village which has given it its name, just on the opposite side of the *gave*, but for quite a distance up and down that bank. In fact the particular vineyard where that most famous drop of Jurançon was grown is situated at Gan, the birthplace of Corisande, wisest, noblest, and most loyal of all the Vert-Galant's mistresses.

This earthy introduction to life was followed by a country childhood ten miles up the *gave*, at Coarraze. It was not quite as homely as the description *jeunesse paysanne* implies. The family with whom he lived was amongst the greatest in Béarn: one tower of their château still stands. But it was simple and free. No other crowned head of that age ever knew what it was to play, in old clothes and bare feet, with boys of his own age as an equal, and to enjoy the same plain country fare as they did. But then no other crowned head could have declared with such sincerity that his ambition was to see every household amongst his subjects enjoying its *poule au pot*.

Most of the instruments of agricultural life he saw all about him as he grew up were little different from those so well displayed by the *Musée de Béarn* in the château of Pau. And the flocks of sheep and herds of cattle which each spring were driven through Coarraze on their way from the lowlands up towards the fresh pastures appearing from under the retreating snows, were heralded then as now by an improvised but never discordant music of bells.

The casting of these bells was then undertaken by any local blacksmith. But experience proved that specialization led to a far superior and more durable product. Specialization has now proceeded so far that a single small family business has an unintended monopoly in bells throughout the Pyrenees.

Jean Dabon, probably already a blacksmith, moved in 1795 from Orthez to Nay, a large, prosperous village just across the *gave* from Coarraze. The sheer excellence of his work has given his descendants the whole vast market. For his bells were not made merely for a lifetime. His great-great-grandson, in the unpretentious premises which would hardly accommodate a small jobbing builder, showed me bells dated 1813 and 1820, which had only recently returned to their place of origin after a century and a half of service, and which were serviceable still. The one dated 1813 had been 'returned to the works' in 1913 for repairs (carried out by another Jean Dabon) to the lip against which the clapper had been striking for a century.

'They are made by exactly the same process which has been in use since Gallo-Roman times. We are now the only casters left in the French Pyrenees, and before the war we used to supply all the Spanish Pyrenees as well. We still sell many there, despite the high cost of French labour, and the fifty-five per cent Spanish duty, because our bells are better than any made in Spain.' (This I had myself often been told in the valleys on the other side of the frontier.)

'We are developing yet another market now in the Alps. Altogether we have two hundred and fifty different models, although we now no longer make the *grelots basques* for sheepdogs, for which demand has slackened.'

'You can by all means write about our business,' he concluded. 'But please don't tell your readers to come and see us. We just haven't got time to deal with them.' So look instead at the bells in the *Musée de Béarn*, or in the *Musée des Pyrénées* at Lourdes. They have all come from the same place!

We have seen how the immigrants from the rest of France find in Pau a *douceur de vivre* of an even more compelling quality than that of the Mediterranean *Midi*; and how the Béarnais themselves look on it as their own dear capital, where the valleys and the *gaves* meet the Vic-Bilh (as they call the *coteaux* to the north). There is yet another, and unexpected, way of approaching it: as a blond pilgrim to the origin of one's royal house.

For Jean Bernadotte, who became King of Sweden in 1818, was born in 1763 at No. 5, Rue Tran, in which his family occupied a single floor. The whole building has now been turned into a Bernadotte museum, and fills one with a delicious sense of wonder at the unlikely story, and its total success.

When their own royal family was in danger of dying out, the

Swedes had plenty of others, of irreproachably Teutonic origins, to choose amongst. Nor would candidates have been lacking, as the monarchies later established in the Balkans were to show. They picked instead a commoner from southern Europe for the best of possible reasons: that he had proved himself not only a brave but a generous opponent. After defeating them at Lubeck in 1806 he carefully looked after the Swedish wounded, and favourably impressed the Swedish officers who came to negotiate with him.

Adopted by Charles XIII of Sweden in 1810, he showed his loyalty to his new country by turning against his old master, Napoleon, who had refused to listen to his advice. Sweden's reward was Norway, and he succeeded to the dual crown in 1818 as Charles XIV. Every generation of his family has included a Princess Désirée, perpetuating the name of his wife, that *marseillaise* beauty of the First Empire.

None has shown anything but pride in their descent from a none too prosperous advocate at the tribunal of the Sénéchal of Béarn. Many of the kings of Sweden, as well as their subjects, have made this *retour aux sources*. The museum is arranged with Scandinavian good taste; and the floor where the family lived gives a good idea of a *béarnais* town home of the later eighteenth century.

But the most nostalgic of all views of Pau must be that of the English. Here we can relive with sad pleasure an age when Britain was so all-powerful, so self-confident, that an empire covering a quarter of the earth was not enough to contain us; an age when we could effectively take over a distant foreign city and create there a microcosm of Victorian society.

It all began when Wellington's army marched across Béarn after the battle of Orthez in the spring of 1814. It was the first time this countryside had seen fighting since that terrible Catholic invasion of 1569. But the inhabitants were surprisingly friendly. They preferred soldiers of whatever nationality who paid for every crumb they took to their own troops who, in the Revolutionary tradition, 'lived off the land'.

The British officers, for their part, liked what they saw.

'The people here receive us well. I have never had greater kindnesses. The mayor prepared us an excellent dinner, and the inhabitants came out of their homes to offer wine to our soldiers.'

'The population is in every respect well-disposed. They overwhelm us with their kindness.'

'In several villages we were welcomed by the inhabitants bearing branches covered in leaves as a sign of friendship.'

'This countryside is beautiful: I could live here and perhaps even forget England. We danced again this evening: the mayor and his wife, tired of waiting up, confided their daughters to us. These were delighted to stay. They sat on my knees and I gave my heart to the eldest who is lovely.'

Many had been away from home for seven years. They felt out of touch, as well as out of pocket, when they were suddenly retired on half-pay after the Armistice. The thought of all those thicker-than-English coverts sheltering game, of all those swifter-than-English streams teeming with trout and salmon, of all that fat, inexpensive poultry in Pau market, drew some of them back to the province where they had been welcomed almost as liberators.

Pau was then only a little town of some eight thousand inhabitants. Its steady growth for the next hundred years was largely due to the arrival of more and more English residents, until they formed a colony of between three and four thousand. To the English influence was due, too, the quality of its growth. Pau had the first modern sewerage system in France. Thenceforward the drinking of its excellent water never presented dangers to the tender Victorian stomach.

The Romantic love of mountains was fed by the building of the Boulevard des Pyrénées along the top of the escarpment above the *gave*. From this on the frequent clear days the main chain of the Pyrenees, forty miles to the south, seems only a quarter the distance. The Boulevard led to a Winter Palace which provided a setting for the main public events of the 'Season', when the colony was further swelled by temporary exiles from the English climate.

Not only the town itself, but the villages round about were affected. For many of the English preferred country life. There they even had the bay of hounds and the huntsman's 'halloo' to make them feel at home, as the only fox-hunt in France met at Morlaas, or found at Ger.

This was the age when Tractarians and Evangelicals were engaged in battles royal, and had the means to sustain them. So the colony had four different places of worship: three Anglican, catering for various brands of churchmanship, and a Church of Scotland for residents from north of the border.

Nor was it exclusively made up of the upper classes. For when everything British was so clearly best, English tailors had to be brought in to cut the colony's suits, and English chemists to supply it with trustworthy British medicines.

It has found its place in literature. Trollope makes one of his characters dream of making a love-match and going to live in Pau on his private income of £800 a year. As recently as between the Wars several of Dornford Yates's novels are actually set there. And with the poet Alfred de Vigny's marriage to Lydia Bunbury of Pau the English colony had its influence on French literature, too.

Though it would be inexact to say that not a wrack remains of all the tea parties and the balls, the villas full of good cheap *béarnaises* maids, and the promenades and perambulations along the Place Royale and the Boulevard des Pyrénées, there is certainly very little left.* France is no longer cheap, and exchange control has killed off a certain way of life amongst the English abroad even more completely than amongst the English in England. Even ten years ago the colony was down to forty. I remember the widow of the last English chemist dying at an advanced old age. All but one of the churches have been sold, and that one receives only a monthly visit from the energetic 'Chaplain for South-West France' at St-Jean-de-Luz (he looks after the Anglicans in fourteen

---

* Joseph Duloum, in *Les Anglais dans les Pyrénées*, traces the decline of the English colony at Pau from as early as the mid-1880s. He makes the point that if the Boulevard des Pyrénées had been opened earlier than 1895 it would have been called Boulevard des Anglais.

9. The remains of Sauveterre-de-Béarn's fortified bridge, where a princess underwent a terrifying trial by water

10. The thirteenth-
century fortified
bridge across the
Gave at Orthez

departments!) The 'English Tailor's' is under French management. And no English members ride to the *chasse au renard*, although the hunt itself miraculously survives.

Yet I have met men, not yet old, who remember how glad they were to take jobs in English houses and gardens when Béarn was less prosperous, and Pau less busy and unfriendly than today. My most poignant experience of this sort was unexpected.

Accompanying a group of British tourists on the train to northern Spain in the late 'fifties, I noticed that one black-haired, dark-skinned girl had an unmistakably *béarnais* name. When I made a discreet enquiry she replied in a strong Scottish accent.

'Me fairther came from a place called Orthez, somewhere in the south of France. He went to work in the stables of a rich Scottish family at another place called Pau. His employer asked him to go back to Scotland with him, to train horses. That's where he met me mother, though they weren't married long before he died. It would be interesting to visit Orthez, though I'm not reelly quite sure where it is.'

I told her that we would be only forty miles away when we stopped at Bayonne, and that it would be quite easy for her to go there and back during a day while she was on holiday in San Sebastian.

'I don't think I will, reelly. You see, I've come for the holiday. It's all a long time ago. And after all, I don't speak any French.'

3. UP THE VALLEYS

We have already seen how important was the carrying trade across the Pyrenees for medieval Béarn, and how several viscounts of that period were more active in the affairs of Aragon than in those of France.

For their subjects it was the same. As late as the seventeenth and eighteenth centuries many Béarnais emigrated to Spain and the Spanish colonies. One even became Governor of the

Philippines. Another made a fortune planting sugar in the Caribbean, and married his daughter to the Président of the Parlement de Navarre (i.e. the Chief Justice of the Court of Béarn), who could thus build one of the few eighteenth-century town houses in Pau, and a country mansion at Gelos.

Two hundred years earlier the Aragonese Pedro de Sacaze travelled in the opposite direction. The Renaissance house he built out of the colossal fortune he made at Nay is still the village's finest monument.

There is nothing corresponding to this traffic in men and merchandise anywhere else along the Pyrenees, even amongst the Basques and Catalans who bestride them, and where they are least an obstacle. Nor is Béarn a particularly 'Pyrenean' state: its 'frontage' on the chain is in fact less than any other old pre-Revolutionary province. Its share of the mountains consists of little more than two long valleys, with no tributaries of any significance.

But these two valleys lead to the two most direct and practicable passes between Roncevaux to the west and Perthus far to the east. The outstanding characteristic of the central Pyrenees is their continuous unbroken height. Their occasional breaches (*brèche* is the name actually used more than once) are only a few hundred feet lower than their peaks, and require almost as much mountaineering talent to scale.

The Somport and the Pourtalet on the other hand, both less than 6,000 feet, are easily negotiable. Moreover, unlike Roncevaux and Perthus, which simply join Basques to Basques, and Catalans to Catalans, they unite two different and complementary regions.

I well remember my first crossing of the Somport, on a tiny motor cycle. I left Jaca surrounded by the scorched stubble of upper Aragon, baking in the late afternoon sun. Miles away across the Aragon valley I could make out every detail on the face of the rocky Peña de Oroel.

Two hours later I was travelling through a very different landscape. The foothills of Béarn were green and damp, and hazy even before evening summoned the mists from the deeper, more urgently flowing streams. There were forests on every side, and an indefinable nostalgic scent of the north. In less than fifty miles I seemed to have travelled most of the way from Africa to Scotland.

Trade comes naturally between areas which are so distinct, with correspondingly distinct products and economies.

The two passes had a further importance for Béarn. Being only eight miles apart, they enabled an army to cross the range in two columns, and to concentrate with less delay than if spread out over many miles, like Charlemagne's when his rearguard under Roland was trapped in Roncevaux. This was one reason for the success of Gaston Phoebus in establishing his neutrality and prestige during the Hundred Years War; for the Black Prince depended on this route when he led an army to dethrone Pedro the Cruel of Castile.

Close together though they are, the valleys of Aspe and Ossau, as they are called, lead quite separate lives. It is thirty miles down from the passes, and only five from Oloron, before a steeply winding road joins one to the other.

It is at Oloron, as we saw, that their two *gaves* meet. The journey up both begins with a short narrow gorge where a glacier once ended, continues through a broad glacially-rounded valley which contains most of the population and monuments of interest, and ends in the steep but exhilarating climb to the pass.

The first place of interest in Aspe after passing its gorge, the Défilé d'Escot, is Sarrance. It owes its octagonal church tower and two-tiered cloister to a miraculous medieval statue of Our Lady. Both are in quiet seventeenth-century country style, so that they formed no part of the Sarrance where a hundred years earlier Marguerite d'Angoulême wrote part of the *Heptaméron*, a *risqué* work inspired by Boccaccio's *Decamerone*. From this 'Marguerite des marguerites', the sister of François I, her grandson Henry of Navarre inherited his claim to the throne of France, and perhaps also his tolerance and many-sided approach to life.

Aspe was later to produce a writer of its own. Cyprien

Despourrins was born at Accous, then the valley's capital, in 1699. Although he spent the later part of his life at St-Savin in Bigorre, he belongs wholly to Béarn. Not only did he write in *béarnais* during perhaps the least favourable period for the cultivation of regional languages. His poetry—unusually again for his period—springs directly from his native heath. No one who has travelled up the Aspe can condemn as mere pastoral formality:

> *La haut, sus las moutanhes*
> *U pastou malourous*
> *Sedut au pé d'u hau*
> *Negat en plous*
> *Sounyabe au cambiament*
> *De sas amous.*

> *Up there beneath the mountains,*
> *An unhappy shepherd,*
> *Seated at the foot of a beech tree,*
> *Drowned in tears,*
> *Was pondering the inconstancy*
> *Of his loves.*

For the everlasting hills to which Despourrins lifted up his eyes under Louis Quinze were the same as those which four centuries earlier had inspired that skilful ruler and fine poet Gaston Phoebus:

> *Aqueros moutanhos*
> *Que tan hautos soun*
> *M'empatchon de bede*
> *Mas amous oun soun.*

> *Those mountains*
> *Which are so high*
> *Prevent me from seeing*
> *Where lie my loves.*

We have remarked that neither valley has important tributaries. Aspe's most interesting is the little Gave de Lescun, along which a steep narrow road leads up to the village of this name. It has a place both in geography and in history.

For Lescun stands magnificently at the base of our first *cirque*. This formation, typical of the central French Pyrenees, is due to the past action of glaciers. It may be defined as an abrupt semi-circular wall of mountains surrounding an almost level upturned basin. Often it is further embellished by waterfalls. The very height of the wall sometimes obscures the peaks above, although not here, where amongst others appears the Pic d'Anie, the first true mountain in the range, which marks the end of the Basque country.

In saying earlier that Béarn saw no fighting between 1569 and 1814 we were deliberately shutting our eyes to another short invasion. For six thousand Spanish regular troops, backed by a further two thousand five hundred militia, had hardly stolen across the frontier when they were forced to retreat at the 'Battle of Lescun' by a mere thousand volunteers and peasants. The date of 6th September 1794 is significant: it was a moment when the 'nation in arms' was busy winning victories against professional armies in every corner of the French hexagon. But the peasants of Lescun were fighting also for Béarn.

The Somport itself, among Pyrenean passes second only to Roncevaux in legend, has had even more practical and economic importance. For the Béarnais it has always been a route rather than a barrier. Today the young *palois* (citizens of Pau) drive a few hundred yards across the frontier each weekend to the ski-slopes of Candanchú. And the nearby ruins of the 'hospital' of Santa Cristina date from as long ago as 1108, when this hospice or refuge for pilgrims to Compostela was built by Viscount Gaston IV of Béarn.

Yet for all the Somport's importance, it is its twin pass, the Pourtalet, that we shall remember longest. The very fact that it is five hundred feet higher is a point in its favour for the unhurried traveller, who will find even more to interest him as he climbs gently up Ossau than he found in Aspe. And throughout his journey he will have the incitement of an increasingly familiar and enlarging shape appearing and reappearing at the end of the valley.

'Le pic du Midi d'Ossau est le symbole de la montagne béarnaise.' It owes this merited apotheosis partly to its visibility from afar, partly to its being the highest mountain wholly within Béarn, and perhaps most of all to its characteristic and immediately recognizable shape. Its cigar-like silhouette draws us even from the Boulevard des Pyrénées at Pau.

I have approached it more frequently from Pau than along the *gave* from Oloron, for the good reason that the road passes the home of Cedric Dannatt. Almost single-handed this happy expatriate has preserved into the second half of the twentieth century something of the English presence in the Pyrenees. He discovered them on holidays from his Paris business in the golden 'twenties. By 1930 he had bought this château on a steep *coteau* above the little Néez, which after retirement became his permanent home.

In the surrounding chestnut woods platforms have been built from which to shoot the pigeons as they migrate each autumn up the valleys. The bookcases within are stocked with one of the best collections of Pyrenaica in private hands. But the mind of the presiding genius is better stocked still, with half a century's memories of climbs here, walks there, places visited and people met, not only in the Pyrenees themselves, but throughout the region covered by this guide.

The position of former capital held in Aspe by Accous is occupied in Ossau by Bielle, in whose fifteenth-century church stands the chest which held the valley's written privileges or *fors*. Here too, and at Laruns eight miles on, the valley still gathers for major festivals such as that of Our Lady on 15th August, when one of the most colourful local costumes in the Pyrenees is taken out of mothballs.

If you cannot synchronize your visit with one of these gatherings, you can only admire the short red jackets of the men, and the long red skirts, shawls, and capes of the women in the Musée de Béarn at Pau or the Musée des Pyrénées at Lourdes. For in the French Pyrenees, unhappily, there remains no valley like that of Ansó, on the Spanish side, where a few old men and women still wear their traditional costume every day.

One thing you *can* enjoy in Ossau, however, is a delicious crumbly white *ossalois* cheese.

Laruns is now three times the size of Bielle. Its church is modern, but there is one of the twelfth century across the *gave* at Béost. Nearby was quarried the marble for the statues of the Place de la Concorde and for the Madeleine, now restored to its pristine Pyrenean purity by Monsieur Malraux. Marble from the Pyrenees has always travelled far afield. It was used for the finer monuments of Roman Bordeaux. At St-Philibert-de-Grand-Lieu right up by Nantes there is a Carolingian tomb in marble from St-Béat near Luchon, which also provided the stone for Trajan's column at Rome.

Just above Laruns a road runs off east through the spa of Eaux-Bonnes, and on up to the Col d'Aubisque. It gives us the opportunity to discuss two topics which will recur from now onwards: the transversal Pyrenean passes, and Pyrenean spas.

The isolation of Aspe from Ossau by a line of high summits running at a right angle to the main chain is paralleled by similar barriers until we are almost within sight of the Mediterranean. In building a road as close as possible to the frontier, for reasons even more touristic than strategic, the French have therefore had to make use of passages even more difficult—but often even more panoramic—than those followed by the roads over into Spain. The most difficult of all, as may be expected, lie within the department of Hautes-Pyrénées. The Col d'Aubisque, it is true, is just inside Béarn. But the really nerve-racking part of the drive comes later, when the road winds round the top of one of the sheer-walled *cirques*, such as we saw at Lescun.

The engineering of this *Route des Pyrénées* is superb, like everything else built by the *Ponts et Chaussées*. But try to avoid its passes in bad weather. For you will not only expose yourself to a slight but needless risk. More important, you will miss the views.

The spas are legion, and I must apologize if someone's favourite watering-place gets left out of this book, as it assuredly will. We have already visited Cambo and Salies, and there are others such as Dax up in the Landes. But it is where the mountains rise up that mineral-rich sources, fed by waters subjected to volcanic and geological pressures, and to chemical action due to those pressures, really begin to proliferate.

They need no help from me, however. The traveller through peaceful countryside who suddenly finds himself amidst the crowds of Capvern or Amélie-les-Bains may well wonder if some time-machine has taken him back half a century. Throughout the summer the *stations thermales* are filled with a selection of quaint survivals from all over provincial France. Contemporaries of Suzanne Lenglen, still in the hairstyles and fashions of the 'twenties. Peasants with wide moustaches under their berets, whose dark suits might be those they stepped into on demobilization in 1919. Long-retired *fonctionnaires* of the *SNCF* or the *PTT*. Ancient schoolteachers with all the *manies* of their profession.

In every country such groups as railway and post office pensioners are the new poor. How can they afford to come here? And why should they choose these inland spas, rather than the coast?

The short answer is 'Sécurité Sociale'. Once a spa's therapeutic virtues have been officially approved—and the smallest and most marginally valuable *stations* seem to be accorded this *agrément*—those taking the cure get all or most of their expenses refunded from the various autonomous *caisses* which constitute French National Insurance. The wealthy can get them allowed against tax. So when it pays to take the waters, what better than combining one's holiday with the mild imbibing of *eaux iodées-bromurées* or *sulfatées calciques* in the shady parks of Argelès-Gazost or Barbazan?

This means that the departure of the English has caused no

11. Lescun with its *cirque*

12. The tiny fortified village of Larressingle might have come straight from a scene in an illuminated manuscript, or some French or Italian primitive

13. The geese of
Gascony: *pâté
de foie gras d'oie*
in the making

14. Tapping the resin
in the Landes on
the traditional
stilts

15. The lake of Hossegor stands for all those *étangs* set in the pine-forest a few miles behind the SilverCoast

16. The basket-work *chisteras* in action on the *fronton* of Hossegor

economic distress to Bagnères-de-Bigorre and the other *stations* where they were so prominent during the great days of their colony at Pau. The Pyrenean spas are prospering, as English spas have not prospered since the fashion for them went out in the last century.

Often their situation enables them to offer modern visitors more energetic distractions than the walks through beech and fir woods under the shadow of the Pic de Ger which so delighted the Empress Eugénie at Eaux-Bonnes. For their hotels make useful bases for winter sports enthusiasts. The ski-resort of Gourette is only five miles up from Eaux-Bonnes, while Barèges over in Bigorre is so high that it doubles as *station thermale* and *station de sports d'hiver*.

Most of them, with the notable exception of the greatest of all, Bagnères-de-Luchon, have few buildings earlier than the Second Empire. But they were in use long before then. Thus, while Henry of Navarre's estranged Queen Margot was taking the waters and other pleasures at Bagnères-de-Bigorre and at Encaux, he was living with one of her ladies-in-waiting at Eaux-Chaudes.

Eaux-Chaudes, in the main valley, is less closed-in than Eaux-Bonnes, and is an even more convenient centre for exploring upper Ossau. I personally, like hundreds of French campers and caravanners, have always preferred a better 'centre' still, camping free and 'wild', *sauvage* as they call it, on the common lands above Gabas, the last village. Here the busiest excursionist will find enough to last him a long week.

There are lakes to be visited, from the artificial but beautiful reservoir of Fabrèges skirted by the main road, to innumerable natural tarns high up in the mountains to both east and west. For climbing men there are these mountains themselves: this is one of the most convenient points from which to approach the Balaïtous (the Spaniards call it the Marmoré), our first peak to top three thousand metres.

Lesser mortals can enjoy both a mountain and a lake with no exertion by taking the cable-car a mile beyond Gabas up the

Pic de la Sagette. It deposits passengers four hundred feet below the actual summit, which remains therefore mercifully unspoilt. Nor does the narrow-gauge railway—claimed to be the highest in Europe—which takes them another six miles on to the lake of Artouste, below another and yet more imposing *cirque*, seem an eyesore. It is only on a *fête nationale*, when the crowded red-painted little train comes into view with its excited, screaming passengers, that one wonders if a section of Battersea Fun Fair has been transported to the Pyrenees.

Whether we camp for weeks in upper Ossau, or merely make a brief halt, the memory of one mountain will remain with us forever. It is appropriate that the slopes of the Pic du Midi d'Ossau should have been declared a nature reserve, which now forms the heart of the *Parc National des Pyrénées*. This stretches along fifty miles of frontier in Béarn and Bigorre, joining the reserve of Ossau to two others, south of Cauterets, and high up to the east of the Pic de Néouvielle. Thanks to the strict laws, strictly enforced, 'le symbole de la montagne béarnaise' now has the fauna it deserves: six hundred of the sure-footed mountain goats or isards, martens, genets, foxes, wild boars, the Pyrenean desman (a kind of water-mole), and a whole catalogue of birds in danger of extinction in this region, such as the grouse-like Grand Tétras. Best of all, a family of bears has now made its home there.

The long narrow French National Park is continued beyond the frontier by an even vaster Spanish one, centred on the valley of Ordesa. The animals recognize no frontiers. Lynxes, still not extinct on the Spanish side, have found their way into France. In doing so they enjoy the best of all views of the Pic du Midi d'Ossau; and it will pay us, too, to prolong our journey right up to the Col du Pourtalet.

For one of the unusual and pleasing features of the French Pyrenees is the way that notable peaks, all the way from La Rhune overlooking the Atlantic to Canigou within sight of the Mediterranean, stand right away from the main chain. At the very frontier, therefore, we can turn back north, to face the mountain we have come to know so well since we first descried it from the Boulevard des Pyrénées.

4. NORTH OF PAU

Béarn started life eleven hundred years ago as a Gascon dependency, and geographically the countryside north of Pau is simply an extension of Gascony. Crossing it from east to west 'against the grain' of its watercourses gives the same difficult 'switchback' type of journey as crossing Gascony in the same direction. A steep climb from the valley of one insignificant little river is followed by an equally steep descent into the valley of another. These streams run on out of Béarn across the Chalosse to empty themselves into the Adour. On bridges we are hardly aware of crossing we glimpse such names as Luy de Béarn, Luy de France, and three separate tributaries of the Léez.

The word for the slopes which line these valleys is the same as in Gascony: *coteaux*. Almost the only feature which differentiates the *coteaux* of Béarn is a wine named Pacherenc. A humble cousin of Jurançon, a little lighter in strength and in its amber shade, the grape from which it is pressed is grown in small quantities: a *clos* here, a corner of a *vignoble* in the next commune. It is quite unknown to commerce, and one only becomes aware of its existence by a scribbled announcement in the window of a café: PACHERENC DE NOS COTEAUX.

Yet the long centuries of Béarn's independence have left their memory. Morlaas, only seven miles north-east of Pau, was its capital after Lescar and before Orthez. Apart from the early charter called the 'For de Morlaas', and the coins from the viscounts' mint which flourished here, it preserves from those years a church with a crowded but much-restored Romanesque doorway. (There is a better preserved one at Sévignac eight miles north.)

Fifteen miles further east Montaner lies in the middle of an isthmus of *béarnais* territory, separated from the rest of the

Pyrénées-Atlantiques by two *bigourdan* islands (belonging to the Hautes-Pyrénées). Gaston Phoebus defended Montaner by a magnificent red-brick castle. Its circular ramparts, surrounding a tower rising a hundred and thirty feet over woodlands and *coteaux*, give us the measure of the forceful fourteenth-century ruler, of whom I dreamt as I lunched and sunbathed at its foot.

Montaner's church is also large and interesting, as is the fortified church of Lembèye a few miles north, though neither finds its way into the guide-books. But for the most part this is a countryside of tiny if frequent villages, with equally tiny places of worship.

Such is Aydie, the north-easternmost hamlet of the department. Its modest 'big house', facing directly on to the road along which the village straggles for an uncrowded half-mile, was the home of Joseph Peyré the novelist. He never married, living there with his brother and sister the life of the cultured provincial, varied by long journeys to the Spain where some of his best books are set, or elsewhere in Europe.

He was in Venice when I called in 1960, and it was his sister who showed me round his book-lined study redolent of flowers, with its view of the beloved *coteaux* he described in his evocation of his native department: *De mon Béarn à la Mer Basque*. It was sad, eight years later to find the Peyrés' manor with a shuttered and unlived-in look about it. His brother and sister, I learned, had died and the writer himself had for a month been in hospital in Pau.

I have described earlier how my long periods of leisure from work based on San Sebastian first enabled me to explore north of the Pyrenees. Though long, these periods were limited, and I began them exhausted. The *coteaux* round Aydie and of southern Armagnac were as far in this direction as I ever penetrated.

I used to stay at Garlin, a large village just off the main road from Bordeaux to Pau. Although it does not seem particularly old, it has always been the centre for this corner of Béarn, and was one of the five places in the viscounty allowed a Protestant *temple* between 1620 and 1685.

North of Pau

Quite by accident I came across the *Hôtel du Parc* there, the very first evening I drove into this unknown land. Full pension was then (in 1960) twelve francs a day. Breakfast consisted of a tall pot of coffee, a new loaf of bread, and about half a pound of butter. Lunch and dinner were each five courses, with *vin á discretion* thrown in. Bed was a deep dream of down, facing an ancient *armoire* across a polished chestnut floor.

Yet during meals one could watch television. Freda White had a lot to say against this practice, and rationally I must agree with her. But she was lucky enough to learn French when she was young, and when going abroad hardly required even a passport. I grew up during the War, when psychologically the Channel was wider than the Atlantic. Then it was possible to half-believe an old coal-miner alongside whom I used to work, who asked in all seriousness: "'Ow d'yer know there's a place called France? Ave yer ever been there? It may just be somewhere that *they've* made up!'

My twenty-second birthday had passed before I first landed in this never-never land, and I can still never suppress a thrill in the realization that it does really exist. And having always been bottom of my class in French (I even failed the absurdly easy French Oral in the old School Certificate examination!), I experienced a constant wonder as I sat in Garlin, the only Englishman for many miles, surrounded by and talking to French people, eating a meal which only a Frenchwoman could have prepared, and even watching and enjoying a French television programme.

It was all so far not only from the England I had left behind, but from the urgent trains on which I worked each weekend, and from the crowded coast where I would otherwise have spent my leisure. Here was a deep rural peace, but a peace quietly pulsating with prosperity. Already many of the farms had cars or tractors. When the *Hôtel du Parc*'s second dining-room was opened up for a wedding party or a visiting *quinze* (Rugby is the great game of the south-west) this prosperity took flesh: *jambons de Bayonne*, *pâtés* of every sort, *canards gavés*, unimagined presentations of pork and veal. I felt like Vasco da Gama in India, or Marco Polo in China.

One thing else excited me. We were close to the borders of three other departments. The cars which pulled up by the *parc* were as likely to have number-plates ending in 40 (Landes), 32 (Gers) or 65 (Hautes-Pyrénées) as in the 64 of the Pyrénées-Atlantiques. Far though I had come from the 'Basque sea' to the north of Béarn, immense new provinces now lay tantalizingly beyond the reach of my five-days-at-a-time leisure.

Chapter 3

GASCONY

I. ARMAGNAC

'Armagnac' has a lovely sound. And it is one of the most evocative words in the French language. Depending on whether one is in historical or alcoholic mood, it brings to mind either that slightly mysterious party which opposed the Burgundians in the civil strife of the early fifteenth century, or 'a special kind of cognac' equally mysterious in its precise origins.

Both the faction and the spirit have in reality the same earthy roots. But these are nowhere near the Île-de-France which was the scene of the clashes between *armagnacs* and *bourguignons*. And they lie a hundred and fifty miles south of Cognac.

Armagnac as a region is little known because it has generally gone under other names. It was the heart of the vast duchy of Gascony which a thousand years ago covered more than half the area treated in this book. As the title passed to the distant kings of England, and as Béarn, Bigorre, Comminges and the lordships of the Landes went their separate ways, 'Gascony' was applied in a more limited sense to this heart, the rulers of which were the Counts of Armagnac.

At the Revolution this region retained its unity. But it was rechristened the Gers, after the most insignificant of all the streams except the Loiret which gave their names to French departments. The very fact that so few people have any idea where the Gers lies shows how, quite undeservedly, it is neglected.

79

The grapes which give the *eau-de-vie* are only grown in the two-thirds of the department which lie to the north and west of Auch, the capital. Like the region of cognac, this is delimited. There is the *Grand-Bois* between Villeneuve-de-Marsan and Eauze. There is the slightly less reputed *Ténarèze* centred on Condom, and extending over the departmental border of Lot-et-Garonne. And there is a wide band of lesser growths corresponding to cognac's *bois ordinaires et bois communs* to the east and south. Leaving the south-easternmost corner of this to the next chapter, we shall concentrate here on the true armagnac country, north of Auch.

It is hard to compare armagnac as a drink with cognac. It is *sui generis*, different. Those diners-out who insist with an air of superiority on an armagnac when their companions contentedly take whichever brandy is brought them, are guilty of a mild if pardonable snobbery.

But the countryside from which it comes is in every respect preferable. Around Cognac it is rather flat, rather unfriendly, and rather uninspiring. Armagnac, on the other hand, is hilly and full of surprises. And it is warm: in its climate, in the character of its people, and in the golden stone from which are built so many of its villages.

Just as golden, and even more warming, is the precious liquid itself. The quiet little town of Eauze, once capital of the Roman province of Novempopulania (nine tribes), is the best spot to taste it. In its *chais* or warehouses mature the finest of all the growths. They are all small, family businesses, glad to show a visitor round, and to sell him a bottle or two at wholesale price.

None of these little businesses have household names to match the great houses of Cognac. It is only comparatively recently that they have bottled the spirit under their own labels. For the region lacks the direct access to the sea which Cognac enjoys down the River Charente. For a long time wine-merchants of Bordeaux bought up everything distilled from its vineyards, and the ultimate consumers were often unaware that the nectar they were sipping was armagnac. Even this anonymous appearance in world commerce only dates from when certain of the meagre

18. Château Lafite, at the heart of the great vineyards of the Haut-Médoc

17. Europe's largest sand-dune: Pyla near Arcachon

19. Ste-Marie-de-Campan on the upper Adour in Bigorre

20. Floating through the caves of Bétharram

Gascon rivers were rendered navigable, and when the first railway lines spread out across the heavy Gascon clay, under the Second Empire (a great period for the south-west, as we have said before).

Yet visiting the Musée de l'Armagnac at Condom, which shows us everything from the instruments used to cultivate the vine, to the regulations for its export, we shall see exhibited documents of 1438, 1439 and 1461 which specifically mention *eau-de-vie*. 'As the above documents prove, armagnac is the oldest French superior spirit of wine [*le plus ancien alcool de vin français de qualité*], it is the only one able to furnish such titles of nobility.'

Soaring into a poetry it would be churlish to condemn, the museum continues:

Rome introduced wine here, then the vine;
The Celts bequeathed their perfect coopers' technique;
The Moors by the intermediary of Spain taught the secrets of distillation;
Gascony offered the wood of her forests,
The bark of her cork-oaks,
The ochre sand of her coteaux,
The mildness of her climate.
This exceptional union is at the origin of armagnac.

The dates 1438 and 1439 belong to the last part of the Hundred Years War. Then the Armagnacs, under their Count, led one of the parties whose civil strife enabled the English almost to conquer France. Yet it was they also who prevented that conquest. For the assassination of a Comte d'Armagnac in 1418 by the Burgundians turned his followers against the Burgundians' English allies.

Thenceforward a long list of *seigneurs*, traditionally vassals of the English king in his capacity as Duke of Gascony, became the closest collaborators of Joan of Arc. One of them, Poton de Xaintrailles, led the single brave attempt to rescue her from prison. For English and Burgundians, indeed, *la Pucelle* became *l'Armagnacaise*. And after her death they continued the struggle until at Castillon in 1453 English rule in the south-west ended forever.

The Gascons admire her still. Her statue, no longer so popular elsewhere in France, still occupies the most prominent place in most Gascon churches. A dear little girl of ten with whom I became friendly when camped at Lavardens asked me one day: 'C'est vrai, n'est-ce pas, que Jeanne d'Arc entendait des voix?'

It is of this period that we shall constantly be reminded as we explore the province. In a vaguely literary sense Gascony conjures up first the age of Louis Treize. It is true that d'Artagnan was born at Lupiac, fifteen miles south of Eauze. But as that sensitive Gascon author, Joseph de Pesquidoux wrote: 'The d'Artagnan of *The Three Musketeers* was conceived at Paris, the Cyrano of the famous scene, who sighs and elaborates on his passion, was born beside the Loire, not the Adour. . . .' In fact the seventeenth century rarely forces itself on us, and the eighteenth only at Auch.

But the Middle Ages, crumbling perhaps, and neglected, yet unspoilt as nowhere else, greet us at every turn. The best-known medieval survival in the Gers—and even that hardly famous— is the tiny fortified village of Larressingle in a field four miles west of Condom. Behind its gold-brown ramparts, almost as high as the width of the space they enclose, it might have come straight from a scene in an illuminated manuscript, or some French or Italian primitive. Moat, drawbridge, towers, keep: it is all as left by its builders and as weathered by six centuries.

Larressingle gets few enough visitors. But Armagnac's other fortified villages get fewer still. One stumbles on them unawares: Ste-Mère a few miles north of Lectoure, with a gate, tower and church forming an ensemble at one end of the decayed ramparts, and a large ruined castle at the other; Terraube, on a sideroad between Lectoure and Condom, its two deserted streets running along the hump of a crest, with an arched gate at one end near a château with grounds maintained almost at pre-war English standards; Tillac away to the south beyond Mirande, which within its restricted limits boasts already the *cornières* or arcades of the later bastides.

Of these bastides there are plenty, founded by both French and English to encourage settlement and to protect their marches. Miélan, Mirande, Fleurance, Valence-sur-Baïse: the list could go on for many lines. Defensive though their character, what has survived is less their fortifications than their regular 'chessboard' plan, with central square surrounded by *cornières* only relatively less ancient than Tillac's.

One of the attractions of the bastides was the freedom they conferred. Those who settled there were relieved of their serfdom. They needed no lord. The best of the Gascon castles are therefore found dominating insignificant and unfortified hamlets. This is the case with the hundred and thirty foot donjon at Bassoues where the fourteenth-century Archbishops of Auch, to judge from the interior, enjoyed by no means uncivilized holidays in the country. Such is the vast pile of Lavardens, built by the thirteenth-century Counts of Armagnac, transformed in the sixteenth century by Marguerite d'Angoulême, and again two hundred years later. After long neglect it is now again being restored.

There are smaller castles marked only by a few ivy-covered walls in the middle of a field. 'It was built by the English' assured the retired tobacco-planter who had found the ruins of the château of Tauzia included with the farm he had purchased near Condom on his return from Madagascar.

Above all, of course, there are the churches. Heading these are no less than three former cathedrals. That of Eauze, like so many churches nearer Toulouse, is of brick, with an octagonal tower. That of Condom, massive without but surprisingly white within, is very late Gothic, with a cloister of the same period. It has a good fourteenth-century chapel, and an organ of 1605. That of Lectoure, a quiet little town high above the Gers fourteen miles east of Condom, is a pleasant mixture of styles from the twelfth to the seventeenth centuries. The adjoining museum contains thirty-four altars on which bulls were sacrificed to Cybele; and there is a thirteenth-century fountain 'of Diana' which also has Gallo-Roman origins. The large church of Fleurance, six miles south, has a fine façade beneath its five gables. Inside are three stained glass windows attributed to Arnaud de Moles who worked at Auch.

Romieu in Gascon means pilgrim. It was for pilgrims to Compostela that Cardinal Arnaud d'Ax founded a collegiate church and cloister in 1318, in a fortified village called La Romieu eight miles east of Condom. It would make just the right setting for a little summer school.

The twelfth-century Abbey of Flaran, five miles south of Condom, is now private property. The old lady who owns it turned a visit which in any case would have been interesting into a voyage on another plane.

'The smoke on the walls of the church dates from the Wars of Religion, when the monks were tied to the pillars and burned. It took three years to burn them all. There used to be three hundred, and when the Revolution came there were only six left. My family did all they could to save the monks: we have always lived near here. And since the Revolution we have done all we can to save the church.'

Certainly both church and cloisters are in good order, with roof intact. In the nave stood an antique tractor, two cars of 1950-ish vintage, a wine press, and several big barrels of wine. She pointed at a huge vat in a side-chapel as the one used by the monks. She assured me that the single column supporting the sacristy, and the columns of the chapter house, were of marble from Carrara. Entering the cloister, she began to explain the capitals:

'That's the founder of the monastery: you see he has a fringe and is wearing a Basque beret. These are dragons, which had their heads cut off in the Wars of Religion. This is a *vache du pays*, with its bell.' Turning to a detached capital: 'The trefoil of the fourteenth century, with a laurel crown of the twelfth century above it. They shouldn't have done it, but of course the poor monks were worn out by then.'

A zodiac-like sign above the door from the cloister into the church she described as the Cistercians' sign. And pointing to marks on certain stones of the church's pillars she remarked:

'Each monk put his sign so that his work could be distinguished. If he'd done it right he got his supper. If he hadn't he went to bed hungry.'

Her involvement with her abbey is to be commended, though I doubt whether she will ever receive the annual award of Pierre de la Garde.

This brilliant journalist refers again and again to the Gers in his famous radio programme *Chefs d'oeuvre en péril.* His theme is that France is Europe's richest country in monuments of the past, yet is tragically neglecting them. His aim is to persuade local groups or individuals to 'adopt' tumbledown châteaux, abbeys, cottages, and to restore them either as homes, or simply as a hobby. His method is by visiting one such 'adopted' monument in each weekly programme, and by awarding a prize each year to the most successful and enterprising restorer. His fear is that vast numbers of 'masterpieces in danger' may be lost only a few years before every one of them will be desperately needed.

For in the age of leisure barely twenty years ahead, 'the Stockholm business man will thankfully fly off on Friday afternoon for a week-end's rest in his château in the Gers.' If, that is, the château in the Gers is still standing.

Any neglected châteaux by the Loire have long since been rescued by the *Beaux-Arts.* Even the forgotten châteaux and *chaumières* of the country of the 'Three Rivers' have been adopted by notabilities as different as Josephine Baker and President Pompidou. But in certain architecturally rich peripheral provinces the situation is desperate.

A glance at Gascony's demographic history explains both this architectural richness, and its present danger. At the beginning of the Hundred Years War, just before the Black Death killed perhaps a third of the inhabitants of Europe, while England had a population of about four million, France had no less than nineteen. Even today France has fewer big cities than any other major nation; and in the Middle Ages nowhere except Paris even approached six figures. The population was not only more dispersed, but it was dispersed more evenly. Upper Provence,

Auvergne, and much of the south-west were then absolutely, as well as relatively, more densely peopled than today.

In 1774, when the total population of France was some twenty-five million, 320,000 of these lived in Gascony. Today, four years after the birth of the fifty-millionth Frenchman, only 185,000 do so. This means that in the past Gascony had more people, who needed more buildings, and had the resources to put them up. Today its smaller population has difficulty in maintaining them.

This demographic decline was due above all to a low birth rate. That between 1870 and 1940 the population of France actually fell, while those of all her neighbours were rising, is often quoted as an example of decadence, of 'Why France fell'. For myself, sprawling all day by a Gascon stream, or parking without difficulty in a Gascon town on market day, it seems yet another reinforcement of her claims to be the most civilized society on earth.

But the low birth rate, combined with a certain amount of emigration to Bordeaux, Toulouse and Paris from a province with virtually no industry, left the Gers empty indeed after the blood-letting of the First World War. Farms were actually going out of cultivation. And so in the 1920s the phenomenon of Italian immigration, long familiar in Provence and the Dauphiné, became known here too. Now every *commune* has its Grassi or its Rosso. They have integrated well into their host society. My little admirer of Jeanne d'Arc at Lavardens was named Jacqueline Trucchi.

Depopulation accentuates the universal shortage of vocations to the priesthood. The diocese of Auch contains not only many Italian, but also a number of Dutch curés, driving round anything up to half-a-dozen scattered churches to say mass each Sunday.

The congregation in each will be of a respectable size, even if mainly female. For this is not a region of wholesale 'dechristianiz-ation' like the Beauce or the Hérault, though there are a few anti-clerical pockets. Maubourguet on the middle Adour and Masseube on the upper Gers were indicated to me by a Dutch priest as being in this category.

That handmaiden of anti-clericalism, left-wing politics, has had more success. Even Communism enjoys a following amongst these peasant farmers. What would the kulaks have thought of a poster at the 1968 general election proclaiming the Party's 'Défense de l'exploitation familiale'?

Whatever its sincerity, the psychology behind the message was sound. For the family farm remains, as it has always been, the basis of Gascon society. In a sense the individual household is even more isolated here than in the Basque country. There was no sea, there were no smugglers' routes across the mountains, to establish links with a wider world. The sticky yellow clay of the Gascon soil impeded communications. The construction of a single good road in 1743 from Toulouse to Auch, Mont-de-Marsan and Bordeaux in itself sufficed to stimulate the development of a rustic Gascon art, notably in furniture, and to fill the farmhouses of Armagnac with the porcelain of Samadet in the Landes.

'Chacun chemine en Gascogne avec sa parcelle d'argile attachée à sa semelle. Every Gascon travels with his bit of clay stuck to his sole.' But the word *parcelle* means 'plot' as well as 'piece', and the saying can be taken to refer to his pride of ownership, as well as to the clinging quality of his soil. Bad communications combined with inborn prudence and proprietor's pride lead to polyculture. By planting a bit of everything the failure of one crop can be balanced against the success of another.

Geography too incites in the same direction. The valleys of the little rivers are close together, so that the average farm running down the *coteau* offers a variety of exposures and elevations. One *parcelle* lends itself to corn, just as another *parcelle* is ideal for vines, while the water meadow at the bottom would be wasted on anything except cattle. And closer to the house will be the pigs; and the geese, ducks and hens which are the province—and the private income—of the Gascon wife.

Where, as in the majority of cases, these houses stand on their own in the fields, the most important figure in any household's life is the nearest neighbour, *le premier voisin*. It is he who is called upon on the many occasions when mixed farming requires cooperative effort, and who is repaid in the same coin. He has a great role to play at the *fête du cochon*, the joyous annual killing of the pig. And, more than any cousin, his presence and support are relied on at the supreme moments of birth, marriage, and death.

The Gascon family whom I came to know best, however, lived in a village, albeit a tiny one. So small that when Gérard Lavalette married Marie Lannux the whole of Aurensan was invited, and easily accommodated at trestle-tables set out in the minute schoolyard.

They were the son and daughter of two of the principal farms, so that she had no difficulties of adaptation. The parents-in-law with whom she moved in were already known to her from childhood. The tasks at which she now worked alongside her mother-in-law were the same ones at which she had always helped her own mother.

Most of these tasks were familiar to me. But I was intrigued to see her *gaver*, forcibly feed the ducks and geese. And I relished the *confits*, various meats preserved in the goose grease which is one by-product of the process. (Another, of course, is *pâté de foie gras*.)

I was treated to a taste of these with white wine when, while camping at Aurensan, I was invited in the evening to watch television in their vast kitchen-cum-living-room, a social centre for much of the hamlet. *Le petit écran*, the little screen, had of course been one of the major changes in their life in recent years. But there had been others.

'The vines need attention,' the old father used to complain to me. For the grapes remained his god, although we were outside the regions of *Grand-Bois* and *Ténarèze*, and although his pleasant white wine had an alcoholic content as low as eight degrees. 'But Gérard neglects the things that really need doing, and spends all his time on this contract work.'

His son knew perfectly well what he was doing. Ploughing a field at Verlus, or clearing some woodland at Projan, he was amortising the debt on his tractor in a quarter the time otherwise required, and at the same time bringing in cash all the year round, instead of merely around harvest. But it was not farming as the old man knew it.

There was a gentle linguistic evolution, too. The old couple conversed together in patois: the Gascon which with Limousin, Languedoc, Provençal and Catalan forms one of the five branches of the *occitan* tongue of the south. Gérard and Marie could speak it, but rarely did. And their two little children were growing up unable even to understand it.

Its disappearance is to be regretted for other than sentimental reasons. For in certain contexts it was more expressive than French. Montaigne himself, when unable to formulate an idea in the language he habitually wrote in, would exclaim 'Que le gascon y aille! Let Gascon get there!'

But its memory will live on, unconsciously influencing the way future generations in the south-west speak French. I noticed some odd genders at Aurensan, and a prominently aspirated 'h'. And what was Marshal Foch's 'De quoi s'agit-il?' before every problem he met, except the Gascon peasant's 'De qué?'

A couple of miles from Aurensan was a tiny spa. There is another, nostalgic in its neglect, at Castéra-Verduzan on the road from Auch to Condom. It was there that as lightning was flashing I heard a sound nearer and sharper than thunder. Guns were being fired against the hail, a danger to the crops against which it is expensive to take out more usual forms of insurance. An old man with a walrus moustache pointed into the clouds with his walking stick: 'They should fire there—there—there!'

The only really flourishing spa in the Gers is at the mud-baths of Barbotan. They stand on the very edge of the department, already amidst the outriders of the Landes pine-forest. Some good restaurants lie on that frontier between pine and vine, notably at Sos twelve miles north-east.

But then one eats well anywhere in Gascony. Moreover one eats one's fill, losing count of the courses as *charcuterie* follows soup, and as cheeseboard follows salad. Forgetfulness is made easier by the bottle of red wine one finds included in every country menu south of the Garonne. And to render oblivion complete one can always round the meal off with an armagnac.

2. THE COTEAUX

Gascony everywhere has *coteaux*. But south and east of Auch, and stretching over into Hautes-Pyrénées (Bigorre) and Haute-Garonne (Comminges), it seems to consist of nothing else. A journey 'against the grain', crossing this countryside from east to west, is as slow and frustrating, as up hill and down dale, as a journey following one of the many valleys from south to north is easy.

Following the 'warp' of this countryside, beside the shallow Baïse up into Armagnac; the gentle Gimone by Simorre and Saramon towards the Lomagne; or the slow Save by Lombez and I'Ile-Jourdain to Grenade on the Garonne, it seems unexciting enough. But a route at right angles, which instead crosses these and other streams, through l'Isle-en-Dodon and Masseube and Miélan for example, is as dramatic a switchback as the English Peak district can offer.

Only the Baïse runs directly from south to north. Its sister streams between the Adour and the Garonne—there are anything between six and twenty, depending on how insignificant are those one chooses to count—fan out to west and east on their way to join the two bigger rivers. The larger of them all rise within a few miles of each other, on the Plateau of Lannemezan, a barely perceptible rise crossed by the main road from Tarbes to Toulouse. It is no more than the rubbish washed down by the Neste d'Aure about a million years ago, and forms no part of the main Pyrenees, or even of the fascinating 'pre-Pyrenees' we shall meet further east. This accounts for the insignificance of these streams, and the incompleteness with which they have worn down the claylands they cross. Very often the *coteaux* of their right banks are much more abrupt than those of their left. Its particular stage of erosion 'gives to the countryside this characteristic allure of Russian mountain'.

The best known, though not the biggest of the streams rising in the Plateau of Lannemezan, is the Gers itself. It rises near the plateau's modest culmination at only 2,120 feet, and runs slightly north-east past the sixteenth-century pilgrimage chapel of Notre Dame de Garaison (i.e. *Guérison,* healing), and the bastides of Masseube and Pavie to bisect Auch.

Auch, capital of the Gers, appropriately straggles down one *coteau* and up another, with the steep hills and commanding views this implies. The best view of all is from the terrace of the late fifteenth-century cathedral, at the top of a monumental staircase which is the legacy to Auch of the Second Empire.

Although fundamentally flamboyant Gothic, both within and without the cathedral owes much of its interest to later periods. The twin towers and elegant porch, closed by wrought-iron grills, belong to the late seventeenth century, as does the magnificent carved organ case.

Even finer examples of woodwork are the Renaissance choir stalls, comparable only to those of Amiens, and with a likeable humanist mingling of figures from the Christian and pagan traditions. Renaissance, too, and of equally high quality, are the stained glass windows of the chapels round the apse, painted in 1513 by Arnaud de Moles. He was born at St-Sever in the Chalosse, and worked also at Fleurance, Simorre and Nay. There are a Louis Quinze pulpit, and a choir screen of 1609. Altogether its cathedral is Auch's greatest museum (though it numbers also an important one of art and archaeology, and a smaller one devoted to Gascony).

One of its minor exhibits is a tomb of 1772, which makes up in human value for what it lacks in intrinsic worth. It is the last resting place of Antoine Mégret, Baron d'Etigny, Intendant of Gascony and Guyenne, and one of the greatest of the royal civil servants who did so much for provincial France under Louis XV. Travellers across the south-west still frequently have reason to remember him, above all at Luchon.

Besides bequeathing to the Prefects of the Gers a working office such as no Ministry in Paris has preserved, he succeeded in superimposing a certain eighteenth-century air on the town where he resided. The wide avenue which leads up from the long square behind the cathedral bears his name, as does the street which joins it at right angles at the town hall. This, too, dates from his time, and contains an exquisite little municipal theatre where Madame de Pompadour would not feel out of place.

But as with so much of eighteenth-century thought and practice, the medieval foundations were never far beneath the polished surface. At the bottom of the hill sloping down to the Gers lies, higgledy-piggledy, an old quarter. Several of its streets formerly led to protected entrances through the city wall, and are still known as *pousterles*, a word directly derived from the low Latin *posterula*, meaning a little door.

For Auch, like all the towns of Armagnac, has a history going back to Roman times. It was then the capital of the Ausci, one of the nine tribes of Novempopulania, whose territory was separated by the River Gimone from that of the Convenae whose city was St-Bertrand-de-Comminges. But this Roman past is buried: only the occasional dim *tour gallo-romaine*, or place-name like Auch itself or Nébouzan, have remained above the surface for a millennium and a half.

The Nébouzan, one of the minor *pays* of Gascogne, stretched north and east of the Plateau of Lannemezan, and took its name from a Gallo-Roman landowner called Nepotius. His villa has recently been discovered on the banks of the Save by the school-master of the neighbouring village of Montmaurin. He also directed the excavations, which have uncovered one of the most extensive and luxurious Roman residences in France.

Its site was known to man long before Nepotius. For at a cave only a mile or so away on the other side of the Save, within the *commune* of Lespugne, was found a Hottentot-like statuette, the 'Venus of Lespugne', which is one of the earliest and strangest examples of prehistoric statuary.

But just as in the northern part of Armagnac described in the previous section, the period which has left the deepest imprint on the land of the *coteaux* is the Middle Ages. Of a journey down the Save, for example, one remembers less Nepotius and Lespugne than the fortress of Laroque, the fortified church of l'Isle-en-Dodon, and the cathedral of Lombez.

Both these last two are in brick, the building material of Toulouse, within whose orbit we are now moving. Both, too, have that *toulousain* hallmark, an octagonal tower in the same material. There has been no bishop at Lombez since the Revolution, yet six and a half centuries ago the then occupant of the see, a Colonna, entertained Petrarch there.

The most impressive of these fortified brick churches, however, is in the adjoining valley, that of the Gimone. Instead of standing at the centre of a market square, like its two sisters on the Save, Simorre rises beside a country road. Its military appearance which Viollet-le-Duc further emphasized when he restored it, therefore stands out the more clearly. The octagonal tower, rising from behind crenellated parapets and five pyramid-crowned lesser towers at the angles, might almost be a central keep. Inside are fifteenth-century choir stalls, sculptures, and stained glass windows, some of which are attributed to Arnaud de Moles whose work we saw at Auch.

Both valleys have monuments of interest downstream from these fortified brick churches. The vast sixteenth-century château of Caumont, 'bosom'd high in tufted trees', overlooks the Save. Several roads were up, cutting me off from it on the opposite bank, and making it seem even more faery-like and unapproachable.

I was more successful in visiting the twelfth-century convent of Boulaur, even more steeply situated above the Gimone. Nuns are once again in residence, and the carved oak stalls of the choir are now in the enclosed section of the church, behind the seventeenth-century wrought-iron grill which separates it from the section open to the public.

Seven miles further down lie the ruins of the Cistercian abbey of Gimont, far more extensive than the guide-books indicate. Chatting with the farmer who owned half of them, I found that he had an interesting point of view.

'If I allowed them to be registered as national monuments, it's perfectly true that I would be given a grant to keep them in proper repair. But then at any hour of the day or season of the year my home might be invaded by the men from the Ministry of Beaux-Arts. But because I don't register them, and therefore cost the taxpayer nothing, why should I have to pay high rates for enormous buildings which don't really lend themselves to farm work?'

Gimont itself is a bastide on a hill above the valley, with a fourteenth-century church and a huge wooden covered market, through which the main road still passes. At the bottom of the hill, and on the other side of the river, stands the chapel of Cahuzac, a pilgrimage centre for much of Gascony. It holds the wooden statue of Notre Dame des Neiges, two centuries older than the late Gothic chapel, itself of 1513.

At another corner of the Cahuzac cross-roads an enterprising canning firm, with the grandiose title of *Les Ducs de Gascogne*, has built a pavilion where one can purchase such tempting local delicacies as *Galantine de dinde truffée, au foie gras,* or *Paté de canard à la fine Armagnac.* The road on northwards leads in eight miles to Mauvezin, with yet another arcaded square, another covered market, another octagonal church tower. And north and west the *coteaux* roll on, through St-Clar and Montfort towards Lectoure and Fleurance above the Gers.

Mauvezin was the capital of the Fezensaguet, one of those forgotten *pays* like the Nébouzan which mean little except to locals or specialists. To mention them all would confuse, and we shall refer only to the Astarac, another *pays* of *coteaux* to the south-west of Auch. This is centred on the market town of Mirande, a bastide whose fifteenth-century cathedral swings a buttress like a loose leg right across one of its streets. There is a small museum with good ceramics and some minor French and Flemish masters. The ruined 'Tour d'Astarac' stands in a lovely leafy site above the Grande Baïse.

Another bastide in the Astarac is Miélan, nine miles south, while the same distance to the east stands Tillac, a fortified village of an even earlier period, to which reference was made in the last section.

The Astarac offers us the choice of two fitting epilogues to our tour of Armagnac and the *coteaux*. On a remote side road between Mirande and Miélan—so remote that even Michelin sites it inaccurately—lies the tiny church of Belloc-St-Clamens. Romanesque murals have recently been discovered there, so that it is kept locked. Of even greater interest, however, is the Roman tomb which now serves as altar. For its carvings of grape-harvesting are the earliest record of *vendanges* in Gascony.

'The grandfather of my husband remembered this tomb being found beneath the old altar, when that gave way,' remarked the veterinary surgeon's widow who had accompanied me with the key. 'And *his* parents,' she went on, speaking as if it were yesterday, 'were married during the Revolution.'

This experience put me in the right, timeless, contemplative mood to enjoy the picnic lunch for which I stopped a few miles further on, beyond Miélan. A particular configuration of the land thereabouts gives to a not particularly elevated belvedere, the Puntous de Laguian, a superb panorama. Twenty-five miles of *coteaux* further back from the range than the famous line of viewpoints through Pau, Montréjeau and St-Gaudens, it commands in all its splendour an even wider sweep of the Pyrenees.

3. CHALOSSE

South of the Adour the department of the Landes rises abruptly into hills which geographically are a continuation of Gascony, of which they once formed part. Though a limited area with a natural unity, these hills were divided into two separate *pays*. The little Tursan, a wine-growing district centred round the bastide of Geaune, included Samadet, where a charming pottery was produced in the eighteenth century. The larger and better-known Chalosse covered all the rest of the area between Aire-sur-l'Adour and Dax.

It is well known above all for its food. For many years, as my work and pleasure took me across the empty pinelands to the north, past the occasional poverty-stricken farmstead, I wondered at the mouth-watering reputation of *la cuisine landaise*. And then I came to realize that this reputation rested not on the flat forest land, but on the Chalosse. On a Sunday I have met families setting off to drive sixty miles for lunch at the famous restaurants at orchard-crowned Amou, or at Hagetmau.

Hagetmau, with the Romanesque crypt of a vanished church, is the most interesting place in the 'interior' of the Chalosse. There are also, however, numerous châteaux and medieval churches (as at Audignon) for those with the time to explore.

The three places of any size lie on the 'edge' of the *pays*, where the Adour divides it from the forest. From Aire, the market town not only for eastern Chalosse and Tursan, but for western Armagnac and northern Béarn, come many of the famous *poulets jaunes des Landes* one meets neatly trussed in *charcuteries* and supermarkets all over France. Thither went the geese and ducks *gavées* by my friend Marie Lavalette at Aurensan.

Aire has two churches of outstanding interest. The cathedral lies in the centre of the town, a few streets back from the river. Basically Romanesque, it has a fine eighteenth-century organ, and a fourteenth-century chapter house whose four vaults are supported by a single octagonal pillar.

A *faubourg* up the steep road to the south called Le Mas d'Aire has a church whose brick exterior seems typically thirteenth-century *toulousain*, with a Last Judgement carved over the main door, and an impressive tower, even if this is square rather than octagonal. Within, however, it preserves six Romanesque arches in the choir, and a crypt of the fifth and sixth centuries. The altar of this crypt is formed by the fourth-century marble tomb of Ste-Quitterie, with some of the earliest known carvings of New Testament scenes. Nearby is a 'fountain of Ste-Quitterie' which no doubt acted as a ready-made baptismal font.

St-Sever, twenty miles to the west, takes its name from another Gallo-Roman saint, to whom is dedicated a more perfect Roman-

21. The Pic du Midi de Bigorre stands away from the main chain of the Pyrenees, so that the Observatory and television relay station on its summit dominate the tangled mountains to the south

22. Looking from the Col de l'Aubisque towards the Pic de Ger

23. Near the Col de Soulor on the *Route des Pyrénées*

24. The time-hallowed approach to the Cirque de Gavarnie for those who prefer not to walk

esque church than either of those at Aire. Some of its capitals are said to resemble those made by Arab workmen in Spain; and in the town hall are preserved other capitals of Gallo-Roman origin.

But the most abiding memory of St-Sever is of the view it offers over the 'sea of pines' to the north. For instead of lying down by the river, it occupies a high promontory above, justifying its old name of Cap-de-Gascogne. Nowhere is the distinction between the Chalosse and the rest of the Landes more apparent.

At Dax that distinction is blurred. The mud baths to which it owes its very name (from the same root, *aquae*, as Aix-en-Provence) are drawn from the Adour. It even throws a suburb across to the right bank. But the main part of the town, still surrounded in part by fourth-century Roman ramparts, lies squarely in the Chalosse.

Though of much more recent construction, the 'Fontaine Chaude' which dominates the square where most visitors arrive has a distinctly Roman look about it. So, perhaps, it should, for Augustus himself came to Dax for his rheumatism. The clouds of vapour which rise from the rectangular basin within this temple-like structure come from hot springs beneath the Adour. Mingling with the river's alluvial deposits they form 'mineral mud', which is given yet further properties by the growth of a freshwater seaweed! There are several more modern spa establishments around the town; and 'patients' wanting a change can try the alternative waters at Saubusse and at Préchacq, a few miles up and down the river.

Dax cathedral, too, has a spurious Roman look about it, having been entirely rebuilt in the classical style under Louis XIV.

From Dax two of the prettiest, as well as most useful roads in the Chalosse run south towards Orthez and Peyrehorade. This last passes near the mill of Benesse, which at only three hundred feet above sea level offers a more varied, if less extensive view than that from St-Sever.

However, the two most interesting places near Dax lie on the other side of the river, strictly speaking beyond the limits set for this chapter. Notre Dame de Buglose is a long-standing pilgrimage centre, to whose ancient chapel and spring has been added a modern church, where Our Lady, a polychrome statue of about 1500 with head quaintly inclined, now resides.

The road there leads past an old half-timbered *landaise* farmhouse, beside a more modern building. In this farmhouse, today converted into a chapel, was born on 24th April 1576 St. Vincent de Paul, the devoted priest who on a different plane did as much as his fellow-Gascon Henry IV to heal the wounds of the Wars of Religion. As a boy he led his cattle to pasture under the oak tree whose hollow trunk still stands alongside.

The Filles de la Charité, the order founded by him, have established here a home for the elderly. Several of these good, sweet sisters came out to chat as I enjoyed a picnic lunch in my motor caravan, smiles lighting up their plain faces and badly-filled teeth. The spirit of 'Monsieur Vincent' had affected even their charges: one dear old lady insisted on giving me a large slice of melon she didn't want. It was with a sense of shame as well as wonder that I drove away from the Chalosse into the empty immensity of the pinelands.

Chapter 4

THE PINELANDS

1. LANDES

Partly because of its classical and Mediterranean associations, partly because even in the north its frequent presence near sand and sea spells sun and freedom, the pine conjures up in many minds a lighter, more exotic image than the solid oak or the Midland elm. And a vast forest of pines, sixty miles wide and a hundred and fifty miles long, seems to raise this image to a higher power.

Mine is one of those minds, and I never approach the Landes without a mounting sense of anticipation. Whether one comes from the *pays basque* or Gascony or over the valleys of Guyenne, one meets outriders, at first single stragglers, and later whole clumps together, many miles before the green sea closes about the suddenly ruler-straight road.

Yet my hopes are never fully realized. That early euphoria as the great trunks rise endlessly on either side; the peace of mind induced by the silence in a lonely clearing; the well-being of waking with lungs breathing resin-rich air—all evaporate within forty-eight hours. Adrift on the green ocean one soon begins to miss the world from which one had yearned to escape.

The simile between forest and ocean is deliberate. For they share a common inhumanity, a lack of one's own kind. Significantly, on the only occasion that I visited the Landes with someone else, we were happy there a full week, paddling our canoe

99

round a lonely lake, and thrilling with the mystery of the single car which in the early hours of one morning sped down the remote road off which we were camped.

The ocean owes its unfeeling quality to its embodiment of untamed nature, the pine-forest to the opposite. For it is wholly artificial: the result of a deliberate plantation during the century following 1788. This took place in two separate stages.

The first fixed the dunes along the coast, hills of sand piled up on the wildest shore of Europe, and moving inland at anything up to a mile a century. The engineer Brémontier, a civil servant who completed under the Republic the work he began under the *Ancien Régime*, first arrested those nearest the sea by a species of grass which threw out a dense network of roots. Behind this cover he then planted the deeper dunes with gorse and broom, which sheltered the infant pines until they were high enough to withstand the constant winds from the sea.

The second stage attacked the vast triangular plain of which this long line of dunes formed the base. Here the problem was different: to break up the non-porous bed of cement-like agglutinated sand a couple of feet below the soil, which prevented drainage and resisted the penetration of roots. The hero here was named Chamrelent, and his solution—deliberate excavation requiring considerable capital—awaited the Second Empire to be put into effect. The American Civil War, which raised the price of resin by cutting off American supplies, made profitable the planting of pine trees. Napoleon III himself purchased and planted a vast imperial estate around Solférino.

The model Victorian village with its church amidst the pines, only a mile from the dead straight Bordeaux–Bayonne railway line, illustrates a number of points about both the Second Empire and the Landes. The church stands for the Emperor's courting of the Catholic vote, the line for all the railway building and speculation which dominated his reign, the name of the village for his adventurous foreign policy, the pines for all he did for the southwest. And that the village needed to be built at all shows how little the Landes were inhabited before the great plantations.

It is the fact that these were made in a largely empty country-side which completes the forest's present inhumanity. Before the nineteenth century it was an unhealthy, marshy waste—*lande*, as the name implies—sparsely populated by *échassiers*, shepherds who to keep their feet dry walked on stilts. The occasional older *landais* farmstead, as we have remarked, is a poor thing of wood and plaster, with little but its age to give it charm. These often used to have a *ristoung*, an opening between stable and kitchen through which the cows could poke their heads.

Even today the thousand square kilometres of the main forest possess only 6,500 inhabitants, or six and a half to the square kilometre. These are the Grandes Landes, stretching from Labouheyre on the main road from Bordeaux to Bayonne, to beyond Roquefort on that from Bordeaux to Pau. Its few villages, like Sabres or Luxey, studies in red tiles and yellow colour wash, seem always more than half asleep. Often the *dépôts de pain* only receive their deliveries of bread twice a week. An identical schematic map on the door of every church tells the worshipper where he can hear the occasional *Messes dans les Landes*.

Though the Grandes Landes exist as a geographical fact, with stated boundaries, they exist also as an image in men's minds. Whenever I have spoken of them, they always seem to be some-where else. 'Those are the Grandes Landes, where one can go twenty kilometres without seeing a living thing,' said the woman near Garein, describing the great fires of 1949/50, which had rendered many people homeless around Luxey and Labrit. But she lived within the Grandes Landes herself.

Into those devastated districts, she told me, had returned a long-absent species. First sighted near Labrit, the wolf had more recently reappeared near Geloux.

One reason for this, and for the lack of protection (now put right) which allowed the fires to spread beyond control, is the Grandes Landes' sheer lack of inhabitants. Even these few have for long been deserting the comparatively unremunerative work of tending the forests in favour of the timber and paper factories which depend on them.

They have now been replaced from an unexpected source. Try 'Bom dia' on the figure you meet collecting the *gemme* or resin from the earthenware cups into which it drips from the incisions in the bark. The probability is that you will be answered by a Portuguese smile.

For the great exodus from rural, interior Portugal, partly to escape from a subsistence standard of living, partly to avoid military service in Africa, and partly in response to a long tradition of emigration which in earlier centuries was directed overseas, has since the early 'sixties flowed towards France. Work in the Landes appeals to these peasants, who are often experienced in the very skills which it requires. For Portugal, too, has its pine forests, including the oldest artificial plantation in Europe (it dates from the thirteenth century).

The lack of inhabitants, and the relatively recent appearance of most of their dwellings, extends even to the capital of the Landes. Mont-de-Marsan takes its name from yet another *pays*. The Marsan is distinguished from the Grandes Landes by the navigable rivers which cross it on their way from Armagnac to the Adour; and Mont-de-Marsan was founded in 1133 at the junction of two of them, the Douze and the Midou. Apart from a few 'Romanesque' houses which mark the line of the twelfth-century ramparts, it has no monuments. What it does offer are the best *courses landaises*.

These are of quite a different nature from the bull-fights—with matadors from Spain—which also take place in the arenas of the south-west, Mont-de-Marsan included. Though the so-called *vache landaise* is a young bull, he is not there to be killed, but to provide a mobile and dangerous 'gym-horse' for the leaps and acrobatics of a skilful, supple *écarteur*.

It seems probable that they originated in the bull contests enjoyed by the Gascon *seigneurs* during the Middle Ages; and they are still held not only in the Landes, but in the Gers, Pyrénées-Atlantiques, Hautes-Pyrénées, Gironde, and Lot-et-Garonne.

Two small towns of the pine-forest are older than Mont-de-Marsan. Roquefort, whose church has a fortified Romanesque apse, preceded it as capital of the Marsan. Labrit has only a ruined *château* to show from the days when it was the seat of the lords of Albret, by which name it used to be known. As it was a Sire d'Albret who married the heiress of Béarn, Foix and Navarre, it is to this quiet village rather than to Pamplona or Pau that we should trace the origins of Henry IV.

For quiet it is, quieter even than Roquefort which lies at the junction of five *routes nationales*. Both, however, seem oases in the unnerving green silence of the forest, here broken only by the still more ghostly charred expanses left by the great fires of twenty years ago.

I am back where I started, yearning for that resin-scented silence, and the self-forgetfulness which goes with it. But not, next time, on my own.

2. SILVER COAST

The ocean's untamed inhumanity is nowhere better exemplified than in the breakers which explode continuously against the wall of dunes dividing the forest from the sea. However silver the sand which gives this coast its name, the continuous beach between the Adour and the Gironde is amongst the most dangerous in the world.

For this reason its little resorts, generally at the end of single narrow roads through the pines, often have something of a make-shift quality. On days of wind or rain their battle with the elements seems a real one. But when the sun shines, and the sand-driving gusts have slackened to a bracing breeze, they are places where it feels good to be alive. Ozone mingles with resin in perhaps the most unpolluted air in Europe.

The sea breeze gives to the sun a peculiar force, so that an *Institut Hélio-Marin* has been established at Labenne near the southern end of this coast, while the largest naturist camp in Europe flourishes at Montalivet up near the northern end. It is not only the largest but the best-organized, open all the year round, and with a full cultural programme during the summer. I

know two Englishmen who practise a form of human trans-
humance, driving slowly down from the Gironde to the Spanish
Mediterranean each autumn, and slowly back to Montalivet each
spring. The Club Méditerranée, too, for long sited at Montalivet
the northernmost of all its seaside holiday villages.

'Naturism', in a fuller sense than that of mere nudity, is indeed
the dominant theme of this coast. Brown feet on pine-needles,
brown bodies against white sand, brown legs crossed on the
terraces of quiet lakeside restaurants, and brown arms propelling
canoes down streams like green tunnels, are the images which
recur whether one remembers the long days on the seashore or in
the interior.

For the Silver Coast, or rather the dunes which are its dominant
feature, have two faces. One is towards the waves which have
created them. The other is towards the wide lakes which they
themselves have created by blocking the passage of the streams
draining the pine-forest. The 'French Far-West', as it is sometimes
called, is a not inappropriate description for an area where a
Californian surf lashes a forest of Oregonian immensity
surrounding lakes of Canadian stillness.

Unhappily the air's freedom from pollution does not extend
to the water of these lakes. They are not deep, and from the lakes
of Hossegor and Léon up to Hourtin (the largest in France) a
hundred miles north, they are bordered by sheltered resorts and
camp-sites busier than those on the exposed beaches. They are
more suitable, therefore, for boating than for bathing.

For they are never cleansed by any tides, their only communication with the sea being by streams called *courants*. These run
fairly fast, because the *étangs*, although so near the sea, lie behind
the dunes at up to sixty feet above sea level. The best-known of
them is the Courant d'Huchet, which empties the Etang de Léon
through a particularly luxuriant stretch of forest. Lucky visitors
at the right season (late July and early August) may glimpse the
flowering of the hibiscus.

Léon is considered by many to be the most beautiful of the
lakes. Biscarosse is probably the best-known. Here in the 'fifties

would land flying boats on a passenger service from England. And here in 1954 was discovered petrol. Oil rigs now make the *étang* look like a miniature North Sea. A free exhibition of the discoveries and methods of production can be visited at the nearby Parentis-en-Born.

Born, as may be guessed, is the name of an old *pays*. Others are Marensin, Maremne, Seignanx, Buch. For recent though the resorts, and virgin the forest, the coastal strip is not quite so free of history as the Landes of the interior. It used to have its ports, though it is now hard to recognize many of them as such.

Capbreton flourished during the centuries before Charles IX diverted the Adour back to Bayonne. Another 'old mouth' of this river was at Vieux-Boucau, whose former name of Port d'Albret shows its ancient connexion with Labrit, miles away in the deep pinelands.

The tower of an abbey which once served as lighthouse, with a Romanesque tympanum, alone survives from the important old port of Mimizan, now buried under the dunes four miles from the sea. On his vast estate near Mimizan the Duke of Westminster used to entertain Winston Churchill.

Most important of the old *pays* was Buch, whose *seigneurs* enjoyed the intriguing title of *Captal*. Le Captal de Buch, sounding like some fabulous monster, is always cropping up in the Hundred Years War, when the successive holders of the title were amongst the staunchest and most powerful vassals of the English. They were important because the lake at the centre of their lands *did* communicate with the sea and *was* washed by the tides. Therefore it could receive the ships which came to load their cargoes of resin, and could also breed oysters. Indeed, it was not an *étang*, but a *bassin*: the Bassin d'Arcachon.

Its oyster beds are still one reason for Arcachon's importance. The other is its situation as the nearest safe beach to Bordeaux, less than forty miles away on a straight, fast road through the forest. It has a *ville d'hiver* as well as a *ville d'été*; for like so many other towns of the south-west it was regarded in the later nineteenth and early twentieth centuries as a winter resort. Like those other towns: Biarritz, Pau, Bagnères-de-Bigorre and so on, it also attracted an English colony. It still has its Promenade des Anglais, and a small Anglican church.

East of Arcachon itself lies La Teste de Buch, from which the *captaux* drew their title, and then a whole string of oyster-growing villages until we reach the resort of Andernos on the other side of the Bassin. It was once a tribal capital, and has the foundations of a Gallo-Roman basilica.

The Bassin is protected from the ocean by a long tongue of land ending in Cap Ferret. This has become a resort in its own right, offering both a wild and a peaceful beach separated by only half a mile of woodland. Facing it on the 'mainland' are two extensions of Arcachon called Pyla-sur-Mer and Pilat-Plage. They are backed by the grandfather of all the dunes along the Silver Coast: the three hundred-foot dune of Pyla, the largest in Europe. A notable *coup* in real estate was carried out by the Frenchman who purchased much of it soon after the First World War at one franc (now less than one centime) a square metre, to the jibes of 'buying desert' and 'building on sand' from his less far-sighted contemporaries.

There is a so-called *Route des Lacs*, the N652 from Capbreton to Arcachon, which wanders a few miles inland past all the southern lakes. Unlike other roads through the pinelands it is very much of the 'Bannockburn by way of Beachy Head' variety. This in itself shows that it is an older route, joining together all the older places we have mentioned.

North of Arcachon the roads, straight once again, run through country still marked by the marshes which once caused the *échassiers* to walk on stilts. The side roads run off from the villages to their coastal offshoots: Lacanau-Océan, Carcans-Plage, Hourtin-Plage, Montalivet-les-Bains. Then the peninsula narrows. Soulac was another old port buried beneath the dunes, from which its twelfth-century abbey church has been rescued. The northernmost resort, Le Verdon, faces on to the Gironde. From the Pointe de Grave, which marks the great estuary's mouth, the ferry-boats ply to Royan on the further shore.

On the last stretch of the Silver Coast, backed by the last dunes and the last pines, stand two great lighthouses. They wink across to the Renaissance lighthouse on the rocky islet of Cordouan (its designer also worked on the Escorial). And other lighthouses wink back from the northward receding coast, where the pine-forest reappears as if it had continued beneath the intervening ocean.

3. MÉDOC

Geographically the Médoc is the entire peninsula between Gironde and Atlantic, up whose west coast we have just travelled. But for everyone except the purist the Médoc means its eastern, inward-looking coast, where on gravelly soils sloping ever so gently to the Gironde lie the world-famous claret vineyards.

An old saying has it that to be worthy of its name, Médoc must come from vines planted in pebbles, and within sight of the great estuary. This does not mean that they must grow in the alluvial soil of the water's very edge. The map of the closely delimited region which alone has the right to produce Médoc shows a band of country some fifty miles long and less than ten miles wide, tapering to a point at Soulac, and always stopping a few hundred yards short of the actual shore.

Two roads run the length of it. The D1 through the edge of the pine-forest is predictably straight. It passes Castelnau, Listrac and St-Laurent with interesting churches, and Lesparre, chief town of the northern or Bas-Médoc, with a square fourteenth-century keep. Just off this road near Castelnau are the Romanesque churches of Moulis and Avensan, the latter with some interesting religious ornaments. Listrac, Moulis and Avensan also number several of the best-known wine-producing châteaux.

The D2, much nearer the coast, winds in and out of the great vineyards of the Haut-Médoc, the southern part of the region. Here lie the *terroirs de haute renommée*, the *très nobles appellations* of Margaux, Saint-Julien, Pauillac, Saint-Estèphe. Here are harvested the great vintages, with their incomparable bouquets. Château Latour, Château Lafite, Château Mouton-Rothschild, Château Margaux, are only the brightest in a constellation of over eighty such estates.

With one or two exceptions—notably Château Lamarque (twelfth to seventeenth centuries), Château Beychevelle, and Château Margaux itself (eighteenth century)—the châteaux are simple dwellings with few architectural pretensions.

Near Lamarque the estuary narrows. It has a minute port from which a ferry crosses to Blaye, and a fort designed by Vauban to protect these narrows.

More important as a port is Pauillac, the real capital of the Haut-Médoc. On its outskirts lie several of the châteaux which have given their name to the best-known vintages. Here is established the *Commanderie du Bontemps-Médoc*, which resembles a medieval guild in its uniforms and ceremonies, and a modern employers' federation in its aims and promotional activity. Even its most colourful occasions, such as the *Ban des Vendanges*— the proclamation permitting the harvesting of the grapes to begin—have a practical link with the trade it supervises and protects. Many aspects of this trade can be studied in the Commanderie's Musée du Vin.

And beyond Pauillac's shady quay stretches, like an inland sea, the great river which enters our region as a swift stream in those Pyrenees to which we must now return.

Chapter 5

BIGORRE AND COMMINGES

I. BIGORRE

The contrast between the Spanish and the French Pyrenees has already been noticed when we were in Béarn. The first are dry, short of roads, and up to sixty miles deep. The second are humid, with excellent communications, and so narrow that barely twenty miles separate the crest from the plain. In Bigorre, the old province which is now the department of the Hautes-Pyrénées, the switchback *route des Pyrénées* runs at only ten or twelve miles from some of the highest peaks, and at the same distance from the fast N117 beyond the foothills.

Where this fast road crosses the N21 from Auch to Lourdes, and the main road up the Adour valley, lies Tarbes, the departmental capital. Badly knocked about in the Wars of Religion, it is a clean, prosperous town, mainly distinguished by the lovely Massey gardens, and by its national stud. Founded by Napoleon to provide his cavalry with mounts (there is a colourful section of the Musée Massey devoted to the uniforms of the hussar regiments), the stud now breeds racehorses.

Marshal Foch, the Allied Commander-in-Chief in 1918, was born at 2, rue de la Victoire, the street named after his achievement. It can be visited. His stubborn temperament exemplifies the Bigourdan, an altogether rougher, less polished character than his neighbour the smooth Béarnais.

Feelings between the two have always been a little sharp. Even in the high tide of liberty, equality and fraternity, Bertrand Barère de Vieuzac, the deputy for Bigorre who on 17th June 1789 proposed that the States-General should be renamed the National Assembly, was also responsible for ensuring that Bigorre became a separate department under his native city, Tarbes, instead of being governed by the Béarnais from Pau. He also, however, prevented the sale of the château of Pau as a *bien national*. Instead he persuaded the Assembly that with its park it should be left to the King as a token of respect paid by the nation to the memory of Henry IV.

That department, like the province, follows the Adour downstream for almost thirty miles below Tarbes, in a narrow strip of land many of whose villages bear the suffix 'de Bigorre' to mark them off from the Béarn and the Armagnac between which they are squeezed. It contains the village of Artagnan which gave its name to the musketeer; and the irrigation channel called the Canal d'Alaric whose unlikely author is said to have been Alaric II, the Visigothic king whose defeat by Clovis in 507 delivered the south-west to the Franks.

One important difference between Béarn and its smaller neighbour was that whereas the first remained independent throughout the Hundred Years War, Bigorre was for much of the time occupied by the English as an integral part of their Gascon dominions. One of the fortresses they garrisoned was the castle of Mauvezin, just off the N117 eighteen miles south-east of Tarbes.

It is very much a château-fort, with a high keep and a square outer wall crowned by towers. Gaston-Phoebus of Béarn, at the height of his power, also ruled here. The inscription over the gate of entry: *J'ay belle dame*, refers to the marriage of that son whom he himself so tragically killed. Appropriately, the castle serves today as the headquarters of the *Escolo Gaston Phoebus*, the society which encourages the study and maintenance of Gascon language and literature.

Within a mile or two are Capvern-les-Bains, the spa where the greatly-mourned actor Fernandel often went for rest and treatment, and the ruins of the Cistercian abbey of Escaladieu. Its later, seventeenth-century additions used to make a charming setting for a restaurant, before their destruction in a recent fire.

Less than ten miles west of Mauvezin, just where the Adour leaves the mountains, Bagnères-de-Bigorre was held by a very different English garrison six centuries later. For from 1830 onwards it was second only to Pau amongst Pyrenean resorts in its number of English residents. In 1840 its *maire* remarked to an Anglo-Saxon visitor that 'Bagnères would attract still more British if he could assure them a clergyman and—*du boeuf*, an article of which the consumption is rare in the mountains.' And from 1852 the clergyman at least was provided!

It was at a boarding house at Bagnères that Selina Bunbury in 1845 sited her *Evenings in the Pyrenees*, a Victorian *Decameron* or *Canterbury Tales*. Six lodgers, to while away the evenings before television or radio, each in turn entertain the rest with a story.

Unlike Pau, it has had no Lacq to give it fresh life since the English departed, and always seems to me a little dead. It has a fine park, and the rivulets which run along the sides of many of its streets are a pleasant feature. But it lacks both the views of the whole range of Pau's Boulevard des Pyrénées, and the closer glimpses enjoyed by the spas which lie deeper in the valleys. For more life we must travel twelve miles west to a town whose career as a Pyrenean resort was barely beginning when Bagnères was in its Victorian heyday.

In describing Lourdes as a resort I have no intention of giving offence. It is a resort as well as a place of pilgrimage, and long before it was either of these it was a fortress, held like Mauvezin during long years by the English. But if you come to it primarily as a resort, as a good place to stay, with plenty going on, and with lovely country in every direction, you are less likely to leave it with exclamations of disgust at 'all the commercialization'.

Of course there is commercialization: medals and souvenirs, Saint Bernadette in every possible material, and grottoes of all shapes and sizes. But the thousands who buy all this rubbish have to stay somewhere, and like to eat well. Yet they are not millionaires. They lack even the affluence of those with *congés payés* on the coast, or with claims on the *sécurité sociale* to cover their cures at the spas. So Lourdes' four hundred hotels and thirty-five camping-sites offer the best value and range of choice of any place in our region.

It has a lake. It has two *téléfériques* and a funicular within a few miles. At Bétharram it has caves. And at St-Pé-de-Bigorre it has a place of pilgrimage eight centuries older than the Grotto itself.

And because it is Lourdes of the miracles, there is always something worth watching to fill those 'Evenings in the Pyrenees'. The torchlight processions, those *serpents de feu* from before the Grotto, winding beside the Gave de Pau and up the long ramp into the upper basilica, are impressive in themselves. They are yet another miracle when it is considered that the individual groups—from Genova, Italie; Motherwell, Ecosse; Liège, Belgique; Limerick, Irlande; as their banners proclaim—have only arrived a few hours before, and are being marshalled by the multi-lingual organizing priests without rehearsal.

The two basilicas above ground, one neo-Gothic and one neo-Romano-Byzantine, may not be to everyone's taste, though they fit the mood of later nineteenth-century religiosity in which Lourdes rose to fame. They were built after the fall of Napoleon III. But as elsewhere in the south-west, he is well remembered here. For he started Lourdes on its way by yielding to Eugénie's entreaties, and removing the palisade erected in front of the Grotto by the Prefect of the Hautes-Pyrénées. Thenceforward it could no longer be said:

De par le Roi, défense a Dieu,
De faire miracle en ce lieu.

But the subterranean basilica, named after Pius X, and opened in 1958 on the centenary of the Virgin's appearance, is in complete contrast. Entering the almond-shaped cream-coloured cavity, so much longer and wider than it is high, one only slowly becomes aware of its size: it can hold thirty thousand pilgrims and wor-

25. The column of the four Evangelists in the cathedral cloister of
St-Bertrand-de-Comminges

26. The château of Foix

shippers at once. It is a daring use of reinforced concrete which enables a single unsupported vault to cover fifteen thousand square yards: the largest such ceiling in the world with so low an angle.

These basilicas make a striking contrast with the little house at 15, rue des Petits-Fossés, where Bernadette Soubirous lived at the time of the apparitions. Her background was provincial indeed: she was only able to understand the Virgin's message because it was spoken in the bigourdan dialect of Gascon:

Qué soy éra Immaculada Counception!'

But then Our Lady already knew the district well. Bétharram comes from the 'lovely branch', in French *beau rameau*, in bigourdan *bét arram*, she held out to a girl drowning in the *gave* several centuries earlier.

The cottage give us a glimpse of an older Lourdes, a humble township huddled beneath its castle. That castle is today its one non-ecclesiastical monument. Its square keep and slit windows sit well, especially when illuminated. And within is the beautifully-displayed Musée Pyrénéen.

There are complete interiors. There are figures showing off the traditional costumes of the valleys on both sides of the range. There are collections of Samadet, and of the coarser pottery from the four centres of Garros, Lahitte-Toupière, Martres-Tolosanes and the valley of the Aude. There are finely-carved ox-yokes, and examples of the quaint 'over-yokes' from which bells used to jingle. There are stuffed birds and animals of every variety. (I was pleased to note that the squirrels caught in 1968 at Laas in Pyrénées-Atlantiques were red ones.) There is a list of prisoners held at the *château* at various times. It includes John Ernault, its English defender in the Hundred Years War, and Lord Elgin, who was interned here for some weeks in 1803.

In the gardens are reconstructions of a number of Pyrenean villages, including one from Upper Aragon. I happen to know Upper Aragon exceedingly well, and found myself unable to place this particular hamlet. Various officials of the Museum appeared with as many different and unsatisfactory explanations. Finally an old Spanish gardener came forward, who had been there when the model was built. 'It's based on Torla,' he said. 'But they added features from half a dozen other Aragonese villages, simply to make it more *típico*.'

A final gallery is devoted to the great Pyrénéistes, those who first climbed and mapped and wrote about the range. The English, largely because of their colonies at Pau and Bagnères-de-Bigorre, occupy a quite disproportionate place in this roll of honour, especially the Leicestershire squire Charles Packe (1826–1896), and the Franco-Irish peer Lord (or 'Count') Henry Russell (1834–1909). Particularly fascinating are the *carnets des cimes*, notebooks in metal boxes. These were left on peaks, where they received entries only from those achieving the ascent, often at long intervals.

It is time that we at last drew near to those summits, towards which all our region turns.

2. HIGH PYRENEES

It was for the best of reasons that the department formed out of Bigorre received the name of Hautes-Pyrénées. It is here that the range becomes an eight thousand foot wall, with passes only marginally lower than the peaks. These peaks, on one side of the frontier or the other, include all the giants of the range save the highest of all. That, the Maladeta, lies opposite the department of Haute-Garonne—for the Garonne is born on its flanks. For convenience, however, we shall treat this adjoining part of Haute-Garonne in this section.

But despite the evident differences between Hautes-Pyrénées and Pyrénées-Atlantiques, the mountains of Bigorre share one thing in common with the mountains of Béarn. Both have a prominent outrider to the north of the main chain with the name of Pic du Midi.

The Pic du Midi de Bigorre lies north even of the main *route des Pyrénées*, midway between the two groups of valleys which make up the mountainous part of the province. The chain of lesser summits which runs south from it make the Col du Tourmalet, by which the *route* crosses this chain at over seven thousand feet, the highest pass along its length. The Col du Tourmalet also enables a four-mile toll road to climb from the pass to within seven hundred and fifty feet of the very summit.

The summit bears a television relay station and an observatory. The water necessary for mixing the cement to build them cost, with transport, over £2 per litre. Simply because of its isolation from the main range it provides an extraordinary view of it. Raymond Escholier said of November, surprisingly an especially favourable month:

'There are then moonlit evenings of a marvellous limpidity. From the Atlantic to the Mediterranean appears the whole chain of the Pyrenees. Alone the summits, by hundreds, escape from the shadows and seem to float, like icebergs, on a polar sea.'

It might be thought that the Col du Tourmalet must have awaited modern engineering before coming into general use. In fact, however, it was from the seventeenth century onwards a short cut to the spa of Barèges from Bagnères-de-Bigorre and places further east. Madame de Maintenon, who was governess to Louis XIV's children before she became his wife, was one of the earliest travellers to use it, along with her charge the little Duke of Maine. The waters of Barèges, seven miles below the pass, were then the most celebrated in the Pyrenees. For their recognized virtues in the treatment of wounds were invaluable in an age before antiseptics and antibiotics. The eighteenth-century military hospital there still flourishes.

At over four thousand feet, Barèges is the highest of four spas in the Lavédan, the seven valleys which fan out south of Lourdes. Coquette Argelès-Gazost treats the veins, calm St-Sauveur women's complaints, and crowded Cauterets chests. Cauterets has more than its fair share of the love stories which distinguished the Pyrenean resorts in the nineteenth century. Chateaubriand suffered here his *ultime tendresse* for *l'inaccessible occitanienne*, and

George Sand her first *frémissement adultère*. And up at the Lac de Gaube Victor Hugo and Juliette Drouet had one of their many escapades.

The Lavédan has several interesting churches, two of which have been celebrated since they drew the praises and the paint-boxes of the nineteenth-century English. St-Savin is a Romanesque abbey church with fourteenth-century fortifications, in a pretty village a little way upstream from Argelès-Gazost. Its organ case dates from 1557. It enjoys a panoramic view of the valley in both directions. The Hospitallers' church of Luz, facing St-Sauveur, is of the same date, but more obviously defensive in character: an ecclesiastical castle guarding Lavédan against marauders from beyond the mountains.

In these mountains, at the head of the Lavédan valleys, lie the two best-known 'sights' of all the Pyrenees.

The western valley, beyond Cauterets, climbs five steep miles past forests and waterfalls to the Pont d'Espagne. From there a stiff climb, or an effortless ascent by *télésiège*, takes one to a plateau at six thousand feet. Along this a level walk leads to the Lac de Gaube.

In 1832 William and Sarah Pattison, a young couple on their honeymoon, were drowned when boating here. The tragedy vested the lake with an added attraction for sentimental Victorians. It caused Richard Monckton Milnes, a friend and contemporary of Tennyson, to break into verse:

> *The marriage blessing on their brows,*
> *Across the Channel seas*
> *And lands of gay Garonne, they reach*
> *The pleasant Pyrenees. . . .*
> *Oh! gaily shone that little lake,*
> *And Nature, sternly fair,*
> *Put on a sparkling countenance*
> *To greet that merry pair;*

But they are a little too careless in the boat . . .

High Pyrenees

One poise too much!—He headlong fell—
She stretching out to save
A feeble arm, was borne adown
Within that glittering grave. . . .

The lake lies at the foot of the mighty Vignemale, the favourite mountain of the Pyrenean pioneer Henry Russell. It is the vision of the main range which makes these two classic excursions, to the Lac de Gaube and to Gavarnie, so memorable. For the Alps, higher though they are, reveal themselves completely, and make no attempt to play a game of hide and seek with their visitor. Approaching the Pyrenees, on the other hand, one line of peaks seems always to give way to another. It is possible to cross the entire range—by the Somport, for example—with hardly a direct glimpse of the crest. It is precisely because in Bigorre the High Pyrenees form an unbroken wall that at certain points one can stand directly below this wall and contemplate it.

Most impressive of these viewpoints are the *cirques*, great bowls hollowed out at valley heads by glaciers which have now retreated. And the greatest of the *cirques* is that of Gavarnie, at the very head of the Gave de Pau.

There are plenty of things to be seen on the lovely road up from Luz. It ends at the village of Gavarnie itself, with its fourteenth-century Hospitallers' church of Our Lady of the Snows, where surely the toughest of all St. James's pilgrims prayed before crossing the snows into Aragon. Some well-known names in the world of *Pyrénéisme* can be seen on some of the tomb-stones in the adjoining graveyard.

The three miles from the village to the *cirque* take a long hour to cover. A profitable ritual has been fostered which argues that it can best be accomplished by donkey. This mode of transport certainly gives the air of a nineteenth-century picnic or a Spanish *romaría* to crowds which would otherwise be distinctly dull. Apart from the commercial motive, the idea that the *cirque* must be approached in a special way is sound.

It is by no means a perfect bowl. There are terraces at various heights where rocks have worn unevenly. It is from the permanent snowdrifts on these, and from the remaining glaciers, that the cascades spring which are one of the beauties of Gavarnie. The largest of the cascades gives birth to the Gave de Pau which we have followed up from Peyrehorade.

But 'bowl' remains a good description. For the *cirque* measures only a little over two miles round at the base, while the surrounding peaks stretch for over nine. The sight of those peaks at sunset has been the crowning moment of many Pyrenean holidays. And it is only appropriate that the famous gap-tooth breach between the Taillon and the Marboré should be attributed, however mistakenly, to the sword of the Roland who at Roncevaux gave the range its greatest legend.

To the east of the Pic du Midi and the Col du Tourmalet lies an even more extensive part of mountainous Bigorre. It is not so much visited, so that you will find greater peace in the fir forests beneath the Col d'Aspin, or among the forty-odd hamlets along the Neste d'Aure. This stream curls west, to rise in the great massif of Néouvielle, comprised now in the French National Park of the Pyrenees. It was naturally endowed with lakes, several of which have been considerably extended by hydroelectric dams.

In less than forty miles, the *route des Pyrénées* goes over three passes. For after the dramatic Col du Tourmalet and the lower but no less inspiring Col d'Aspin, comes the Port de Peyresourde. This offers a less extensive panorama, but has the distinction of dividing Bigorre from Comminges.

The road on down the valley of Larboust towards Luchon passes three Romanesque churches of interest. St-Pé-de-la-Romaine is largely built of Roman materials. That of Cazaux-de-Larboust contains fifteenth-century frescoes. And that of St-Aventin is a unique treasury of eleventh-century sculpture: tympanum, bas-reliefs, capitals and pillars of the porch. Within is a twelfth-century wrought-iron choir grill.

Two very different subsidiary valleys run off that of Larboust. The lovely, harsh valley of the Neste d'Oô runs off south, up to the lake of that name, fed by a nine hundred foot waterfall from an even higher lake. Another waterfall on the way up, called *la chevelure de Madeleine* through its fancied likeness to the Magdalen's tresses, marks the beginning of the Val d'Esquierry, famous for its wild flowers.

Very different, with its chain of little villages and Romanesque churches, is that of the Neste d'Oueil to the north. It offers fine views of the Maladeta at about the same distance on the other side of Luchon.

And so to Bagnères-de-Luchon, most ancient and most elegant of all the Pyrenean spas. Celebrated under Rome, it owes its modern development to the great Intendant, d'Etigny, whom we met at Auch; and in its plan and its leisurely air preserves a certain eighteenth-century balance and order. There are several fine houses of this period, including those which hold the tourist office and the museum.

Hilaire Belloc scorned its comforts. But I find it wonderful that this civilized little city of pleasure should lie at the end of the only road which connects it with the outside world (for the two other roads lead immediately up to passes, and then on to nowhere in particular). Branches of well-known Paris shops, excellent bookshops, luxury hotels, Casino, golf-course, swimming-pools, and that most specialist of cures, treatment for the vocal cords (ideal for singers, barristers, teachers, preachers!) are all crowded into this deep green valley-head beneath the highest peak in the Pyrenees.

It is the Maladeta *massif*, immediately to the south, which offers the most spectacular of all the excursions from Luchon, by the Hospice de France and over the Port de Vénasque, to the Spanish village of Benasque. (Every word hereabouts has two spellings. The Maladeta is sometimes the Monts Maudits. Their highest peak, the Aneto, emerges in French as the Néthou.) By this route can be reached the Trou du Toro, where the infant Garonne loses itself for several miles.

But there are many more excursions. The lovely valley of the Lys is reached by the same road; and from this branches off the motor road to Superbagnères, the ski-resort on a plateau four thousand feet almost directly above Luchon. And we have already visited other places of interest on our way down from the Port de Peyresourde.

There is a much easier way to visit Spain than by foot over the flank of the Maladeta. This is by the road up the little Col du Portillon which marks the frontier, and down to Bosost. Here the Garonne, having re-emerged above ground at the Guell del Jueu, gathers force with every kilometre. By the time it enters France at the Pont du Roi six miles downstream, it is already rather more than the average *gave* or *neste*.

For countless visitors to Luchon, this short trip has been enough to justify their boast of having 'been to Spain'. But Arán, the uppermost, Spanish section of the Garonne, was completely isolated from the rest of Spain each winter, before the construction of the tunnel above Viella (Arán's little capital). Geographically it lies north of the main mountain chain; and until 1192 it came under the rule of the Counts of Comminges. This old province also included Luchon, and a wide area to the north which we shall now explore.

3. COMMINGES

The most famous place in Comminges is the city which bears its name. Yet in a competition for the world's smallest city St-Bertrand-de-Comminges, with barely three hundred souls, would be ahead of even St. David's in Wales. But it is a true city just the same, with a complete city wall, a magnificent cathedral, and an illustrious past to prove it.

It owed its foundation to Pompey, thirteen years before his rival Caesar crossed the Alps. For Provence, the original *Provincia*, was not the only corner of Gaul at which the Romans were nibbling before the great offensive of the Gallic Wars. Lugdunum Convenarum (from which Comminges evolved its name) was therefore a more mature, romanized place in the first century after Christ than brasher, more recent cities further north, like

Bordeaux or Paris. Herod the tetrarch, and Herodias the mother of Salome, perhaps found it a not uncongenial residence when they were exiled there four years after the Crucifixion.

The city they knew lay a short mile to the east of the present St-Bertrand, on the plain behind where the hamlet of Valcabrère straggles beside the Garonne. Excavations have uncovered forum, temple, baths, theatre, and the earliest Christian basilica in Gaul. The abundant discoveries of statues, inscriptions, mosaics, pottery and coins are displayed in a chapel and in an eighteenth-century house up at St-Bertrand.

One corner of the ancient site still breathes a Mediterranean nostalgia. The eighth- and ninth-century church of St-Just de Valcabrère rises behind its cypresses like some mirage from the Appian Way or Ravenna amidst the lush Pyrenean foothills. Like many of the houses of Valcabrère, it is largely built of stones from the adjoining ruins. But it is a work of art in its own right. The God the Father with the four Evangelists above the main door, and the four statues forming columns which support it, are good examples of early Romanesque.

The Gothic wonder which succeeded St-Just as the cathedral church of Comminges rises on the hill behind. I use the word 'wonder' advisedly, for it has not inappropriately been compared to 'La Merveille', the church of Mont-St-Michel. And the situation of St-Bertrand: the isolated little hill, the steep streets, flanked by a choice hostelry or two rising to the crowning marvel, answers well to the description given it of 'Le Mont-St-Michel des Terres'.

Although the essential part of the cathedral: nave, chapels, apse, and the magnificent carved wooden choir stalls, is Gothic, the porch is Romanesque, as is the irregularly-shaped cloister poised above the abyss and looking out towards the Pyrenees. One of its columns, the best-known detail of St-Bertrand, is formed by the four Evangelists standing back to back.

The tomb of St. Bertrand behind the high altar is of the fifteenth century; but the saintly bishop who lies there lived three centuries earlier. About 1120 he became the second founder of the city, which had remained uninhabited since its destruction in the course of one of those fratricidal wars between the Frankish princes in 586. The civilized Lugdunum below, with its baths and spacious forum, had perished earlier still, when the Visigoths reached the Pyrenees in 408.

Yet its memory, and that of the Convenae tribe whose capital it had been, lingered throughout the Dark Ages. It found expression in the county of Comminges, one of those fractions into which the great Duchy of Aquitaine broke up from the tenth century onwards. Including as it did all the upper valley of the Garonne, it lies at the very centre of the French Pyrenees, and in a key position for the region covered by this book. A journey down the river not only carries us the whole length of Comminges, but presents us with several rapid changes of scenery.

Leaving St-Bertrand on our left, and the little spa of Barbazan on our right, we soon find ourselves climbing into the bastide of Montréjeau. This lies on the main N117 from Bayonne and Pau, and like Pau it has one of those panoramas of the main chain of the Pyrenees—here at their highest. A similar view can be enjoyed nine miles on at St-Gaudens, at whose busy market the products of the mountains meet those of the *coteaux* to the north. Although it has a large, restored Romanesque church, there are better examples of this style at smaller places off the main road, like Montsaunès. This name, originally Mons Saliniensis, comes like that of the nearby Salies-du-Salat from the 'strongest' mineral water of Europe.

Back on the main road the traveller's interest is divided between the very recent and the very old. The recent is the purification plant at Boussens, which separates into its constituents (butane, propane, petrol, etc.) the gas found as long ago as 1939 at St-Marcet, eight miles north of St-Gaudens.

The ancient are the Roman survivals at St-Martory (two bridges) and above all at Martres-Tolosanes, with an excavated villa, and with columns and an early Christian tomb in its church. This church already follows the style of Toulouse, with an octagonal tower.

An even better example of this style is the former cathedral of Rieux, which can be reached by a deviation from the main road. This stands near the western end of a fascinating little chain of hills called the Petites Pyrénées, which we shall be exploring in a later chapter.

Then the plain of Toulouse widens. It seems an appropriate place for the forces of north and south to meet, and that is just what happened on 12th September 1213 at Muret, then the capital of Comminges.

The north was represented by Simon de Montfort—grand-father of the first English Parliamentarian—and his land-hungry followers, ostensibly crusading for Catholic orthodoxy. On the side of the south stood not only 'the Albigensians', but the nominally Catholic Count of Toulouse, and the powerful King Pedro II of Aragon, who brought in his train lords like the Viscount of Béarn who had no connexions with heresy whatsoever.

So although in the church of St-Jacques St. Dominic told his beads in the chapel still named after his Rosary, the battle being waged outside the town was not so much between two faiths as between two cultures. The monument erected seven hundred years later, half a mile north, on the road to Seysses, makes no mention of the Cathares. It speaks instead of the common front put up by the speakers of those closely related tongues: Catalan, Languedoc, and Gascon, in defence of the liberties of the south:

'En coumemouraciou ded VII Centenari dera batalho de Muret ount dab ed arrei en Peiro Aragounes Catalas Lengadoucias e Gascous cayoun pera defenso deras libertats ded Meidio'.

4. COUSERANS

We have several times already used the two parallel roads along the Pyrenees: the N117 from Bayonne all the way to Perpignan, which stays 'mainly in the plain'; and the switchback N618, the *Route des Pyrénées*, which keeps as near to the mountain crest as possible. The sole point at which they meet is St-Girons, the only place of any size in the old province of the Couserans (which derives its name from the Gallic tribe of the Consorani).

This early came under the rule of the Counts of Comminges. Although since the Revolution it forms part of the department of the Ariège, the union is artificial. For the Col de Port which divides it from the old County of Foix is at once the frontier between the dialects of Gascon and of Languedoc, and between a green, damp, Atlantic world, and the grudging, dry pastures of the Ariège valley.

Whichever of the two roads we choose, the entry into the Couserans is delicious. The N117 runs up beside the little Salat river, past a number of hamlets on the opposite bank. Then appears a slightly larger village on a hill. The motorist had best change into first gear without delay, for he must negotiate a narrow thirteenth-century bridge, and then engage on the steep climb which leads to the former cathedral.

With the bishop's palace it completely dominates St-Lizier. Basically a massive Romanesque, it has a fifteenth-century doorway and an octagonal *toulousain* tower. Apse and nave are slightly out of line, adding to the primitive feel of the construction. This is completed by a fine twelfth-century cloister with charming carved capitals where Simon de Montfort signed the pact which ensured the defeat of the Albigensians.

The cathedral contains a witty Latin epitaph to Canon Ardingost, who died in 1334. 'HIC JACET IN TUMBA ROSA MUNDI, NON ROSA MUNDA, NON REDOLET, SED OLET QUOD REDOLERE SOLET. Here lies in the tomb the rose of the world who is today withered, no longer giving out perfume, but the scent of the grave.'

Very different in spirit are the other former episcopal buildings. Now housing an old people's home and a lunatic asylum, they are of the seventeenth century, though resting in part on Roman foundations. While the carved woodwork of Notre-Dame-de-la-Sède, the bishops' private chapel—and technically a second cathedral—is Baroque, the charming pharmacy has an almost Rococo air.

Sleeping on its hill, with the river cutting it off from the main road, St-Lizier has retreated from the modern world. It forms an entirely appropriate setting for a friend I visit whenever there. He has retired from a career in North Africa to a world of dreams and illusions, fascinating to listen to but remote from reality. Almost as remote is the nearby village of Montjoie (from Mons Jovis, the hill of Jupiter) to which he once took me. It stands, complete with fortified church, within fourteenth-century ramparts a mere fifty yards square.

For the everyday world one must follow the Salat a couple of miles to where it is joined by the Lez at St-Girons, a pleasant watery little town whose industry consists of making cigarette papers. It is the market to which all the valleys of the Couserans descend. But it can be reached also by one of those valleys, along the *Route des Pyrénées* over the Col de Portet d'Aspet. Although a mere 3,500 feet, this is approached up steep gradients on both sides, and commands views wider than many much higher passes, notably towards the Maladeta, and towards the Couserans' own frontier peak, Mont Vallier.

The valley which runs down from the pass, the musically-named Bellongue, holds 'twelve villages in twelve kilometres'. Several have attractive little Romanesque churches, and in the lowest, Audressein, stands the charming Gothic Notre-Dame-de-Tramesaygues. Inside are statues and frescoes of the fifteenth century.

As recently as 1950 the *Guide Bleu* could speak of 'la Bellongue' as 'très peuplée'. But today, alas, this is only true at weekends or holidays, when the *toulousains* drive up to the *résidences secondaires* they have created out of abandoned cottages. For the Couserans, without any roads into Spain, and without any well-developed ski-resort, has suffered greater depopulation than any other region along the range. Though the old people who are left naturally regret the old days when the village school was full, and the farms all cultivated, they bear no resentment against the newcomers. Indeed, they would be hard put to survive without them, for a friendly lift to the nearest shops from the weekender is often the only substitute for the vanished bus.

Without descending all the way to St-Girons, shops and services can be found at Castillon-en-Couserans, a mile up the Lez from where the Bellongue runs into it at Audressein. It lies beneath a fortified Romanesque chapel, where once the Counts of Comminges had a castle, commanding thus the entry to two valleys. One, known as Biros, is that of the Lez itself. It runs past the little spa of Sentein to remote mines of lead and zinc, and the 1,600 feet deep pothole called the Gouffre Martin, near the frontier.

Shorter and more rewarding is the other valley, Bethmale. It takes its name and its source from a delicious little lake with mossy shores beneath giant firs. But it derives greater fame from the costume once worn by its women, but now only seen on such occasions as the day of Our Lady (15th August) at Ayet, or Michaelmas at Arrien—or, better still, at the Musée Pyrénéen at Lourdes. It consisted of an embroidered velvet bonnet, a striped silk shawl, a brightly-coloured apron, and beechwood clogs. These last had toes pointing upwards in the fashion which came in at the end of the fourteenth century. Imaginative local historians have found likenesses in this costume to those of Bulgaria, and have suggested it was introduced by the Cathares, whose beliefs may have come via Bulgaria from Persia.

At St-Girons the N117 leaves the Salat and swings grandly cross-country towards Foix, with broad bends and sweeping views. It is the *Route des Pyrénées* which follows the Salat valley for a few miles, until this runs off up into the mountains by a narrow gorge. The minor road which continues to run beside the stream can only do so by burrowing through a rock.

It is worth pursuing it, however, for it leads to an even longer series of valleys than those above Castillon. The Salat valley itself widens round the little town of Soueix before following a gorge up to Salau. For seventy years there has from time to time been talk of building a road from here by a tunnel under the pass of Salau into Spain. It would open up not only the Couserans, but the Spanish valley of the Noguera Pallaresa, which has almost lost its through-traffic since this was drained off through the new tunnel to the valley of Arán.

Two of the various subsidiary valleys have strings of villages of their own. That of the Garbet runs from the hamlet of Vic, with its Romanesque church sporting a sixteenth-century ceiling of painted panels, up to the spa of Aulus-les-Bains. Like the other valley, that of Ustou, it ends in a fine wall of mountains, from which the infant Garbet cascades down.

The *Route des Pyrénées*, after it has left the Salat, winds up to the Col de Port through pleasant villages like Biert and Boussenac, with a mere shadow of their former populations. Massat, once the administrative capital of the Couserans, is the only place of any size. I asked an elderly man at Biert where everyone had gone, expecting to hear the usual stories of emigration to the cities, and was surprised when instead he pointed towards the war memorial.

'They can't be in two places at once', he replied; and for the two world wars I counted indeed eighty-one names. Many sounded like notes for an unwritten symphony of the southwest. There were four Auriac, four Dandieu, seven Dagheil, eight Loubet, five Maurette, six Mirouze, eight Piquemal, seven Rivère, and eight Servat.

At the Col de Port itself I received the more conventional explanation from a man barely ten years older than myself, who had driven up a herd of cattle from the other side.

'There are only two of us left in the valley who bother to bring our animals up here now. And there will be no one after us. The young don't want this life. My son works in Paris. But look how the land is suffering.'

And I looked where his hand indicated to where the undercropped pastures were already beginning to waste under erosion, that scourge of highlands which man first deforests, and then deserts.

Chapter 6

COUNTY OF FOIX

I. THE RIVER OF GOLD

Ariège derives from *aurifera*, gold-bearing. Until the end of the last century its waters were panned for dust and nuggets. Within living memory the curé of Luzenac was taken blindfold to administer the last sacraments to a dying Catalan, who with two companions had found the secret of a particularly rewarding stretch of water.

Gold is just about the last thing which would occur to the traveller through the Ariège valley today. Apart from isolated factories converting local deposits, such as those producing talc at Luzenac, or aluminium at Auzat, the picture is everywhere of an agriculture in rapid regression, with tourism only a partial, uneven, and seasonal substitute. The valley of Saurat, leading up to the Col de Port, from which my informant of the end of the last chapter had driven up his cows, is typical with its population of 6,000 in 1782, 3,000 in 1896, and 1,500 today. Typical also are its charming if amateurish attempts to attract summer visitors to quiet camping sites and furnished rooms.

The main valley of the Ariège itself sees plenty of tourists of a very passing kind. For it forms one of the principal routes to Spain: the great N20 which from Toulouse leads by Andorra to Lérida, or by Bourg-Madame to Barcelona.

Metaphorically at least this is a golden road, leading from the great red churches of Toulouse to the sun-baked sierras of the

27. Roofscape of tiles in Foix

28. Corneilla-de-Conflent

Spanish Pyrenees and the yellow sands of the *Costas*. And it has provided many a golden day for one who has often dawdled along it in the opposite direction.

For I have spent many nights in my motor caravan on top of the Envalira pass. The French built a road over it in 1931 at almost 8,000 feet, to provide direct communication with the co-principality whose sovereignty their President shares with the Spanish Bishop of Seo de Urgel. Ludicrously—but helpfully —it is now crowned by petrol stations representing every major oil company of the western world, enabling motorists to fill their tanks at little more than half the French price before dropping to the frontier at Pas de la Casa a couple of miles below.

But at night the attendants go home. There is a wonderful combination of cosiness with exaltation in watching the sun reflected from the snow-covered peaks long after the valleys below are lost in darkness, while eating a hot meal in the warmth of a self-contained home-on-wheels. I only step out into the bitter night air in order to post my last letters with Andorran stamps. These generally include one or two to friends resident in Andorra. Such internal mail requires no stamps, for it is delivered free by either the French or the Spanish Post Offices, which both operate in the principality.

Next morning I have dressed and dropped down below the Customs post soon after dawn, to breakfast on the side of a high steep valley. A tiny silver stream, too far away to hear, almost cascades down its bed far below. This is the Ariège, which is born just inside French territory in the Cirque de Font-Nègre, below the pass. Below where I sit it actually forms the frontier, for at this point Andorra includes several square miles on the Atlantic side of the watershed.

The Asiège is in fact the easternmost river in the Pyrenees whose waters eventually reach the Gironde. But the valley is wholly Mediterranean in feeling: in the colours of its sky, in the scent of its undergrowth, and in the atmosphere of its villages. This last remark is not intended as unqualified praise. For there is a sad, shuttered quality about Mediterranean villages which are neither large enough nor warm enough to cater for the outgoing, open-air instincts of Mediterranean man.

I remember being puzzled when a lady of my acquaintance who was born in the Ariège, but who moved up to Brittany after marriage, remarked one day: 'I much prefer it up here. It is much warmer and more friendly. Down where I come from the windows are always shuttered, and the people never speak.' But I have often thought of what she said as I have walked round the first French hamlet, l'Hospitalet (at almost 5,000 feet), or driven through Mérens-les-Vals six miles distant and fifteen hundred feet lower down the valley.

Not that I have ever been in a mood to be depressed by such thoughts. What I remember Mérens-les-Vals for is the excellent bread I have so often purchased from its old-fashioned *boulanger*. And all introspection is banished when after another five narrow miles the road drops into Ax-les-Thermes.

That *bâtard* at Mérens was our first French bread. Ax is our first French town. And how very French it is! All that is quintessentially Gallic seems concentrated into this exquisite little spa on the edge of Spain. There is a *parc* with green trees which really shade. There are *pâtisseries* with those delicate if expensive cakes, sold by nimble girls in nylon overalls which in their fit somehow hint at *haute couture*. There are mounds of 'Golden' apples, the one fruit which Spain often lacks.

And of course there are baths which give the town both parts of its double-barrelled name. The hottest of them flow at 78° Centigrade into a large stone tank at the side of the main square, first built by St. Louis for returning Crusaders who had contracted leprosy. In taking on enough of this hot water to give myself a bath in my caravan I am committing no sacrilege; for the tank is now used as a ready-made laundry by the women of Ax.

Can you get any more French than St. Louis? I'm afraid you can. Whenever I drive into Ax, fresh from the gnarled dark skins and rough speech of Pallars or the Monegros, a figure crosses the road in front of me, which always seems almost identical.

She is of *un certain âge*, and has the gravity of expression and of

carriage which her years permit. Below a jumper with somehow
fussy edges—an unnecessary pattern in the rib, perhaps even a
suggestion of lace or *brodérie anglaise*—she wears one of those
skirts which prove this to be the one garment the French can
sometimes fail to cut properly. And above the glasses through
which she peers at me as at an intrusion from another planet
her head is crowned by a floppy, broad-brimmed, white linen
hat.

She is the cousin, however many times removed, of the member
of the Women's Institute in some Cotswold village, or of the
Ladies' Bowling Club from Leamington Spa. But she would never
acknowledge the relationship. She knows that she represents
la civilization francaise: and I sometimes wonder whether she
hasn't been posted there intentionally, to remind me that I am
returning to it.

The villages come more frequently after Ax. Near the spa of
Ussat is the cave of Lombrive, within which the last recalcitrant
Cathates were buried alive, more than eighty years after the fall of
Montségur. I am not surprised to learn that a neo-Cathare cult is
now practised there: such is now the fashion for this heresy, until
a generation ago almost forgotten.

At the little market town of Tarascon-sur-Ariège (so called to
distinguish it from the Tarascon on the lower Rhône), the N20
is joined not only by the *Route des Pyrénées* coming down from the
Col de Port, but also by a road from an important lateral valley.
Two miles up this lies an even more famous cave: the Grotte de
Niaux. Now that Lascaux is closed, it is the greatest exhibition
of prehistoric art in France open to public view. The paintings of
horses, deer, and above all bison—many shown pierced by
arrows—are set in a natural gallery, the *Salon Noir*, half a mile from
the entry. They were drawn in a cunning unguent of bison-fat
mixed with oxide of magnesium.

This valley is called Vicdessos, after its stream and its most
important village. Once it was known for its bear-tamers, who
used to spend the winter months touring far afield with their
charges. Within this century one was seen dancing with his bear

at St. Leonard's in Sussex. Today it still leads up to one of the wildest parts of the Pyrenees, beneath the twin peaks of Montcalm and Estats, the easternmost peaks to top the magic 3,000 metres. About 1800 a beautiful wild girl, *une fille sauvage*, lived naked in these solitudes. Captured and imprisoned in the square tower of the château of Pau, she soon died.

Amongst the Romanesque churches along the Ariège are Sabart, originally founded to celebrate a victory of Charlemagne over the Arabs; Mercus on the site of a fortress of those same Arabs; and St-Jean-de-Verges, where in 1229 the then Count of Foix made his peace with the representatives of St-Louis. Foix itself has also its Romanesque church of St-Volusien, though much restored.

But Foix, capital of the Ariège, and one of the smallest *préfectures* of France, is above all its château. Though it shelters a departmental museum of which its guide knows how to make the most, this is above all an unforgettable silhouette. Those three towers on their rock amidst a circle of mountains signal to us from whichever direction we approach them—and not least on the summer nights when they are floodlit. The oldest tower is square, and dates from the twelfth century. Also square, but with a satellite tower at one angle, is the fourteenth-century tower. A hundred years later, however, the science of military engineering had advanced, so that the most recent tower is round.

Only the first of these, therefore, formed part of the fortress which successfully repelled several attacks by Simon de Montfort during the Albigensian Crusade, to surrender finally when the French king himself brought up his full siege train in 1272. After the Counts of Foix became also Viscounts of Béarn in 1290 it was little used, and it is doubtful whether Gaston Phoebus had anything to do with the round, fifteenth-century tower which bears his name.

The largest town in the Ariège is not Foix, but Pamiers, twelve miles downstream. Its cathedral and two other churches are basically *toulousain* Gothic, much restored. But the mingling of stone with the more usual brickwork shows the same meeting of mountain and plain which gives Pamiers the biggest market in the department.

From Pamiers the N20, running straight for kilometre upon kilometre, stays close to the Ariège until it empties itself into the Garonne, almost on the outskirts of Toulouse. The most rewarding place for a halt is just halfway along, at Cintegabelle. Here, away from the main road, an old bridge spans the river near a thirteenth-century *toulousain* church, a mile below where it is joined by a stream called the Hers. In the angle where they meet stands the abbey of Boulbonne, whose reconstruction in the universal brick of the plain was only completed in the first year of the Revolution.

In the Introduction I described how Freda White in *West of the Rhône* declared that 'the road from Carcassonne is the frontier of this book'. This left me an irregular quadrilateral of land between that road, the Ariège, the Aude and the Petites Pyrénées. Spread between three departments, it had made itself chiefly memorable to me for the cold winds which are funnelled up the Aude from the Languedoc plain, and for the brilliant views of the distant mountains which these winds make possible.

I had privately decided to forget this area except for Mirepoix, which is after all in Ariège. It must be the southernmost of all the bastides, with a variation on the *cornières* or arcades round the central square called *couverts*. Here the actual first floors of the houses project to form the 'cover', being supported on wooden columns. The former cathedral is of the fifteenth century: it has a vast nave, and a spire rising more than two hundred feet above the little town. There is a good hotel, which is also the rendezvous of many of the more interesting local inhabitants.

I would also have drawn the reader's attention to the strange church of Vals, halfway between Mirepoix and Pamiers. Partly carved out of a rock, it has a Carolingian crypt, a circular Romanesque tower, and an apse, described as 'Mozarabic', which contains frescoes dated as early as the eleventh century.

But I would have left unmentioned the region to the north and east of Mirepoix. And then, knowing that I was writing this book, a friend gave me a copy of *Cathars and Reincarnation* by Arthur Guirdham.

This fascinating story by a level-headed English G.P. tells the story of one of his patients. As a child and schoolgirl she had dreamt—or 'remembered'—incidents from the life of a Cathare girl living in this very district in the mid-thirteenth century.

They included the names of people we know to have appeared before the Inquisition, places and events for which obscure research can vouch, and even couplets of poetry which a Professor of the University of Toulouse has declared recognizably medieval Languedoc in style and language.

Read it for yourself if you wish to make this rather featureless countryside live, to people it with characters such as the fierce Pierre de Mazerolles, or to take part in the siege and capture of Montréal. Coming to it in the right frame of mind you may even enjoy an experience such as mine at Fanjeaux.

It was here that 'Puerilia' stayed for some time with a Cathare community, in a house which still stands. It is now a convent, and I asked a nun coming out from it whether it had indeed been 'une maison des Cathares'. She grudgingly acknowledged the fact, obviously none too pleased by this reference to a distant heretical past.

Stepping inside the main entrance I found a second large door confronting me, with a semi-circular glass panel above it. Suddenly I became conscious that a face was staring at me through this panel. It was heavy, middle-aged, female, and hooded, with only the eyes showing any expression. There seemed to be no body attached, nor any visible means of supporting a body if it existed. Oddest of all, it was set at an angle of forty-five degrees.

For several moments we stared at each other, and then I left, a convert if not to reincarnation, at least to the intriguing qualities of the countryside immediately south of 'the road from Carcassonne'.

2. PETITES PYRÉNÉES

The very fact that no one else mentions them would be an excuse for me to do so. But this curious chain, almost like toy mountains at less than a quarter the height of the Pyrenees proper, is an experience in itself, with several small, and one major, places of interest.

Freda White hints at their existence when she speaks of 'the Pyrenean level called the "Plantura" because it is forested'. She must have been talking to someone who was used to patois, for in French it is the *chaîne du Plantaurel*. And though it is forested everywhere at the point she crossed it, near Quillan, it is as bare and dry as the countryside it runs through further west, in the Ariège.

This is where it is at its most typical: one, two, and sometimes even three parallel lines of hills, between which run streams and roads. From time to time these streams cut gorge-like passages for themselves, more dramatic in appearance than the size of either hills or watercourses leads us to expect. We went through one of these just beyond St-Jean-de-Verges on our way from Foix to Pamiers.

To the east of Foix there are similar cuttings at La Bastide-sur-l'Hers; between Laroque d'Olmes and Lavelanet; and at Carla-de-Roquefort, where part of the village lies within the walls of the ruined castle. I once spent the night of 23rd June there, helping to feed the bonfire of St. John alongside a Spanish Republican exile, who almost wept with homesickness at hearing my two little fair-haired nephews speaking perfect Spanish, complete with Valencian accent.

To the west of Foix there is a cutting at Sanguet, and another at Pailhès held by a medieval and Renaissance castle; while at Le Mas d'Azil there is a natural tunnel. For a quarter of a mile the river Arize has scooped its way through the chalk, and the Route Nationale 119 has had the good sense to follow it.

So did primitive man. A series of caves leading off from the tunnel can be visited. Do not expect Niaux or Lascaux. Magdalenian—or, to define him still more narrowly, Azilian—man did not paint here. He sculpted and he engraved. And, of course, he ate, leaving behind the bones and teeth of mammoths, bears, reindeer and other animals which have long ceased to roam the Little Pyrenees.

In the third century Christians used one of the caves as a chapel. In 1625 Protestants endured a siege here. The reformed church is still strong in the pleasant little town of Le Mas d'Azil at the northern end of the tunnel.

Because they are so unknown the Petites Pyrénées are quite un-spoilt. At Daumazan-sur-l'Arize I enjoyed the best value in rest-aurant meals I have ever had in France or anywhere else. My mother and I were the only diners apart from a *banquet de noces*, celebrating a wedding which united two prominent local families.

My mother amused herself and entertained me by reciting the imaginary but plausible history of every guest: the bridegroom's aunt who had become buyer for a store in Toulouse, and acquired an extra polish and dress-sense in the process; the bride's two bachelor uncles who had been given places of honour in the hope that in due course they would reciprocate in a testamentary way. And all the while plate followed plate followed plate. For instead of bothering to prepare an ordinary menu just for ourselves, they gave us helpings of each course of the wedding breakfast.

Wine, too, as far as I remember. We were in no mood for remembering much as after paying our bill (8 francs each—and this was as recently as 1968) we at last staggered out to the beds already made up in my motor caravan beside the Arize.

But good wine accompanied by good food leaves no hangover. Early next morning I halted six miles on to buy our *croissants* at Montesquieu-Volvestre, beneath its interesting variation of a *toulousain* church tower, with sixteen instead of merely eight sides. And we had crossed the Garonne and left the last of the Petites Pyrénées behind us before we stopped to prepare the coffee which was to accompany them. We were already back in the land of the *coteaux*.

3. DONÉZAN AND SAULT

Nothing could have been more logical than the way the French created their present departments in 1790. Yet their boundaries still often follow certain lines dictated not by geography or economics, but by chance of medieval politics.

A good example of this is the tiny *pays* of Donézan, half-a-dozen remote hamlets on a mountainside high above the Aude. Surrounded by glorious forests studded with lakes, their only monuments are the Romanesque church of St-Félix, and the ruined castle of Donézan, lording it over the minute 'capital' of the *pays*, Quérigut.

They are only joined to the rest of the Ariège by a hair-raising track to Ax-les-Thermes, across the Paillères pass at over 6,500 feet. Yet the departmental boundary does not even stop at the river Aude. At one point it even throws a bridgehead across it, to include in Ariège the Forest of Carcanet, which once formed part of Donézan.

It would be so much more natural for the people of these hamlets, when they had business with the *préfecture*, to follow the Aude down to Carcassonne. But instead, even in the 1970s, they have to go to Foix—simply because their ancestors were once subjects of the Counts of Foix. Small wonder that during the 1848 Revolution they went so far as to declare themselves the independent republic of Quérigut!

More often than not they go the long but safer way round, through Quillan. Of this road Freda White wrote: 'One road leads off it to the ruins of the Castle of Montségur; if you have the heart to take it: I had not.'

I must recommend readers to steel their hearts and to take that road. I personally feel that the Cathares have been a little overdone recently. They were never more than a minority of the population, even in this western part of Languedoc where they were most numerous. But the ruins of Montségur atop their precipitous cone-like hill have more than their anticipated charisma.

Marilyn Wailes the English painter spent a whole summer

working here, and finally condensed the whole brooding spirit of the place in a small, imaginative oil painting. Against an almost schematic vision of the castle on its hill some of the two hundred and ten '*Parfaits*—the full, 'pure' Cathares who were not even given the choice between death and recantation—are seen at the stake. At one moment they look like white knights at attention. At another they shine like man-sized candles. And so she allows our minds to roam back to King Arthur . . . and forward to Latimer.

A short cut from Foix to Quérigut would take us across another little *pays*: Sault. Although this lies in the Aude, it is wholly Pyrenean, with forests of giant firs, and steep climbs up to the 3,000 feet plateau on which they lie.

The most exhilarating approach to it is from Ax-les-Thermes over the panoramic Col de Chioula. A turning to the left can take one on a vertiginous *route des Corniches* far above the right bank of the Ariège. The best of the firs, which are planted irregularly, and stand unregimented, with the occasional mossy clearing, lie on the D29 which runs down from Sault to the N117 at Bélesta.

This also takes us near the Fontaine de Fontestorbes, which from July to October, if you are lucky, is a *source intermittente*. This means that its considerable outpouring comes in jerks: thirty-six minutes 'turned-on', thirty-two minutes 'turned off'. I was there in June, so that it was unfortunately running all the time.

But whether it is working or not, this is a region not to be missed. At an inn somewhere along that lonely, high, forest-girt N117 I once saw a menu which included wild boar.

Chapter 7

PYRENEAN CATALONIA

I. CAPCIR

Just as at the Col de Port we crossed the linguistic frontier from Gascony to Languedoc, so on crossing from the Ariège into the Pyrénées-Orientales we cross another linguistic frontier, from Languedoc to Catalan. Though these are all members of the great southern family which also includes Provençal and Limousin, and though the transition from one to another is often almost imperceptible from village to village, the line which delimits Catalan has more significance than the others.

For Catalan, unlike the others, shows no signs of dying. The young speak it as well as the old. And Catalan, unlike the others, is spoken in countries other than France. It is the tongue of the five million most commercially active citizens of Spain. It is the official language of the principality of Andorra. It even survives in a corner of Sardinia, where the Kings of Aragon once ruled.

Until 1659 this Catalan-speaking region of France was in fact ruled by the Kings of Spain in their capacity as Kings of Aragon and Counts of Barcelona. Then what the historians often loosely call 'Roussillon' was ceded to France by the Treaty of the Pyrenees. But Roussillon is in fact only the coastal plain round Perpignan. Freda White realized this, and in *West of the Rhône* her description of Roussillon stops short at the Pyrenean foothills.

The Catalan-speaking areas ceded in 1659 included also the

upper parts of four valleys. Each is a little *pays* in itself. Although all adjacent, they offer surprising contrasts in climate.

The smallest, poorest, and bleakest is the Capcir. It is formed by the upper valley of the Aude, and it is poor and bleak because it is not only high, but faces north with the river. Just how high is best realized by those who have followed the Aude all its serpentine and gorge-interrupted way up from Carcassonne. The Capcir at its lowest point is not much below five thousand feet; and the very fact that the slope upwards and outwards is gentle leaves this shallow half-basin cruelly exposed to winds from either north or south. I have been in a snowstorm there in the middle of May.

Its lesser hamlets have a primitive, earthy quality I have met nowhere else in France. Réal at night, as the three or four naked bulbs went on at the corners of the unmade streets, seemed as God-forsaken as some *aldea* of the *sierras* of central Spain. More so, for no children ran barefoot in and out of the shuttered houses: no bar provided a focus for even a minimum of community life.

The only places which count their inhabitants in hundreds are Les Angles and Formiguères, the 'capital'. This has a church of a Romanesque as primitive as the *pays*, with a Christ in wood of the same period.

Some believe that the Capcir owes its even shape to its having once been a lake; and it has certainly lent itself remarkably well to the two artificial lakes which now cover an appreciable part of its area. The lower, that of Puyvalador, is a little daunting in its austerity. For although three hamlets lie beside its bleak, bare banks, they are all like the one described above.

The upper, on the other hand, that of Matemale, is partly framed by one of the lovely pine and fir forests which give the Capcir both wealth and beauty.

Within and up above these forests are other smaller, natural lakes. There are some fifty, all told, on the northern face of the great massif which culminates in the Carlitte at 9,750 feet. That of Balcère is the easiest to reach, and one of the prettiest. Another is the Lac d'Aude, from which the river takes its source. But of course many of them are the sources of streams which never flow near the Capcir. The Oriège, appropriately if confusingly, runs into the Ariège (it gets its name from the same gold-bearing qualities). The waters of the Etang de Lanoux eventually reach the Sègre, and thence the Ebro. And only a mile or two from the Lac d'Aude begins another river, the Tet, which at first follows an exactly parallel course.

It has three distinct stages. The fertile plain of Roussillon is in large part its delta. Its middle reaches, which we shall later be exploring, form the well-defined *pays* of Conflent. But its upper reaches, at between four and five times the average altitude of the Conflent, really form a separate little *pays* on their own.

Generally, however, it is treated as part of the Capcir or of the Cerdagne. There is an obvious reason for this: the watersheds which divide it from these two neighbours are barely noticeable, although the French in their logical way insist on calling them *cols*, passes. Were it not for the plaque: 'Col de la Perche', two miles south of Mont-Louis, one would be unaware that one was leaving the basin of the Tet for that of the Sègre. Likewise it is only a similar notice reading 'Col de la Quillane', four miles north of Mont-Louis, which announces the transition to the valley of the Aude.

Mont-Louis is the centre of this little world. With such insignificant 'passes' it is obvious that it controls the routes along all three valleys: the road up the Aude from Carcassonne, the road up the Tet from Perpignan, and the road down the Sègre into Spain. So, a few years after the Treaty of the Pyrenees, Vauban set to work to build here a fortress, which he called after his royal master. And because the population has never occupied more than a portion of the area enclosed by his walls, one can the better appreciate his design: the *glaces*, *demi-lunes*, *redoutes*, *bastions*, *fossés* and so on of that science of which he was the acknowledged master.

The streets are huddled together just inside the Porte de

France. Until recently it was worth penetrating to the citadel, where an experimental 'solar oven' concentrated the sun's rays. But this no longer functions since the erection of a more powerful instrument at Odeillo.

Of the handful of hamlets in this upper valley of the Tet beside Mont-Louis itself, two are famous in the world of Romanesque. La Llagone, on the road to the Col de la Quillane—at 5,600 feet it is almost at the same altitude—has a twelfth-century wooden Christ.

Planès, up a steep side-road to the south, has a unique triangular 'clover-shaped' Romanesque church. Each 'leaf' of the clover is roofed by a separate little cupola, and these support a larger cupola between them. It is known locally as the *mezquita*, the Spanish word for mosque. But I find it very hard to believe that any Moslems chose to establish themselves on this remote *altiplano* during the eighty or so years when this region was nominally subject to the Caliphs. They had all Andalusia to settle!

Up above Mont-Louis there is not even an isolated farmstead beside the Tet. But it makes one of the loveliest walks or drives imaginable. For five miles it is relatively level. Here its banks form one vast 'wild' camping site, where I have spent many active days amongst the firs, and dropped into deep sleep to the background of swiftly-flowing clear water. Then the road climbs on to a bare plateau, where it ends beside a huge reservoir. A hotel is open here in the summer months.

The name, Lac des Bouillouses, almost tells us that it was largely a marsh before the building of the dam. I was not surprised when my two nephews had the time of their lives catching frogs all morning. Critics can carp at the ecological and scenic damage effected by the *Electricité de France*. To my taste their reservoirs have often improved as well as enriched the landscape. Walking beside the lake at nearly 7,000 feet, with all of French Catalonia below me, I felt in every sense on top of the world.

2. CERDAGNE

Much of the Cerdagne lies even higher than the Capcir. But it faces south, because the Sègre, the river of which it forms the upper valley, flows south-east into Spain. As the massif of the Carlitte protects it from the north winds, and as it is above many of the clouds, it is at once dry and clear.

The northern side of the valley—the side facing south— therefore enjoys exceptional sunshine. The road which follows it is known for this reason as the Solana, and Font-Romeu, where it touches 6,000 feet, is reputed to be the sunniest place in France. It claims 3,000 hours of sunshine a year—as many as Algiers. And just as the Engadine, the equally high upper valley of the Inn in Switzerland, has become both a winter and summer resort, so Font-Romeu welcomes those who come to ski, those who want a healthy summer holiday, and children with weak chests who can attend its *lycée climatique* while they recover.

In 1968 it found a new role, when the athletes of Europe cast around for somewhere on their own continent which offered the rarefied air in which they would have to compete at Mexico. Now a *cité préolympique*, complete with swimming baths, skating rink, and even a submarine centre, stands ready for any teams which require acclimatization before proceeding to high altitudes.

At 6,000 feet, of course, when it is cold it is cold. I remember shivering at St-Moritz in the Engadine in July. And because Font-Romeu is so much more recent than the Swiss resorts with their cosy Victorian past, and has that white antiseptic angularity which characterizes the newer French ski stations, it can sometimes feel even colder than it really is.

On days like that it does one good to walk up to l'Ermitage, the sanctuary of Our Lady of Font-Romeu. The 'spring of the pilgrim' which gives the place its name flows from the wall of a chapel forming one side of a court. The three others consist of rooms for the use of pilgrims.

Though restored in the eighteenth century, the chapel has the air of a much more ancient building. It is dominated by a large, colourful altar-piece of 1707 by Joseph Sunyer. Narrow stairs on either side of this lead to a tiny chamber behind known as the Camaril, a name as Catalan as that of the artist. Here Sunyer has created a golden Baroque jewel, carving and gilding every square inch of wall and ceiling. Within it one feels a long way from the cold world outside.

From near the sanctuary a road climbs to the ski-station proper, with its lifts and *pistes*. One can drive or walk beyond it another couple of miles to the imaginatively-named 'Belvedere 2000' (it stands at just 2,000 metres). From here there are fine views not only back over the Cerdagne and forward to the Carlitte peaks, but immediately below into the upper valley of the Tet, which we visited in the last section.

For most of the year, from her feast day on 8th September until Trinity, Our Lady of Font-Romeu resides not in her own sanctuary, but in the church of Odeillo, a village much older than the ski-resort and a little lower down towards the centre of the valley. There within the eleventh-century Romanesque church she replaces the Virgin of Odeillo, whose statue, it is claimed, was hidden during the 'hérésies cathares' from 1196 to 1205.

Just above Odeillo stands the twenty times more powerful solar oven which has replaced that of Mont-Louis. It cannot be visited, but everything worth seeing is visible from the road. Sixty-two smaller mirrors, swivelling so that they can be trained on to the sun, face south and reflect the sun's beams on to a concave mirror, a hundred and eighty feet in diameter, which in turn concentrates them. Its use is on substances whose transformation requires exceptional heat.

The road south-west along the Solana from Odeillo and Font-Romeu passes through a 'forest' of rocks called the Chaos de Targasonne. Moved there by glaciers, they are the type of natural phenomenon which seems always to appeal to the French. Many visitors will be more interested by the Romanesque church of Ur, and their appetite for this style will be further satisfied by the villages on the other, southern side of the Cerdagne: the 'Baga'.

29. Romanesque capitals and horse-shoe arch at St-Michel-de-Cuxa

30. Chapel in the Vallespir

This side offers one of the best views over the *pays* from the D33, which leaves the main N116 from Mont-Louis just at the Col de la Perche. This is also the best approach to Lló, with one of the finest of the Romanesque churches, and a beautifully-situated quiet hotel. The Romanesque church of Saillagouse, now 'capital' of the *pays*, has been much restored; but that of little Hix, which used to be the seat of the Counts of Cerdagne, has changed little since it was built nearly eight hundred years ago.

The palace of the Counts is recalled in the name of Palau-de-Cerdagne, a little to the south of Hix. This also has a Romanesque church; and in adjacent Osséja delicious pears ripen at over four thousand feet.

Bourg-Madame is the frontier village; and this frontier, more than most, spells history. It was given the name in honour of Madame Royale, the Duchess of Angoulême, when she and her husband returned to France by this route in 1815. As daughter of Louis XVI, and wife of a future Dauphin, she was a royal Madame twice over, and behaved as such. 'Hautaine' is how Larousse sums up her character: at once proud and arrogant. She was one of the reasons why the Restoration lasted a mere fifteen years.

It is a highly artificial frontier. For the Cerdagne is a natural unity, and Puigcerdá, which used to be the capital of the whole, stands on its hill a mere mile from Bourg-Madame. Yet there is a good reason why it runs as it does. By the Treaty of the Pyrenees Spain ceded to France thirty-three villages of the Cerdagne, because this was exactly the number required to place under French control the route round the Carlitte, and so on to Foix.

The Spanish negotiators had grasped at the word village, and insisted that Llivia, as Julia Livia the Roman capital of the Ceretani, and technically therefore a town, should remain theirs. It has in fact even today got a larger population than any of the thirty-three villages, and forms a curious little 'island without water', approached only via Bourg-Madame and Puigcerdá, and back across French territory by a carefully-observed *chemin neutre*.

The N20, following the route thus made available to France, runs up to the Col de Puymorens beside a river called the Carol, through a village called Carol, and beneath the Carlitte massif. Who is this Carl or Carol thus repeatedly remembered? Why, Charlemagne of course, the deliverer of the Pyrenees, still celebrated as its liberator by neighbouring Andorra.

Ruined towers form an attractive but confusing feature of this narrow valley. There are the two thirteenth-century Tours de Carol near the village of Carol, and the single eleventh-century Tour Cerdane up by the village and ski-resort of Porté-Puymorens near its head. But neither has anything to do with the village of Latour-de-Carol much lower down.

Even so, at four thousand feet this seems rather high to have an international railway junction. Here meet the lines from Paris and from Barcelona, and the line from Perpignan: marvels of mountain engineering all three. I have never travelled on any of them. But many times when working at the Gare d'Austerlitz in Paris, hot and tired on a summer night, I have derived refreshment from the mere sight on two or three carriages of that unlikely red on white plaque:

TOULOUSE
FOIX
AX-LES-THERMES
LATOUR-DE-CAROL

3. CONFLENT

The achievements of the railway engineers are at first our main interest as we drop rapidly down the Tet from Mont-Louis. The most remarkable are the Gisclard rigid suspension bridge, and the Séjourné viaduct, both named after the engineers who created them. Commandant Gisclard was killed in an accident while his design, the first of its kind in France, was under construction. Hamlets are tiny and away from the main road, except for three small spas. And then we emerge from a gorge to find ourselves in Conflent, the heart of French Catalonia.

It is central geographically, between the peripheral and much-traversed regions of the Cerdagne and the Roussillon. And unlike the charming but smaller Vallespir, it is large enough and rich enough to have nurtured in its time a confident culture. Pablo Casals, in holding for many years his music festival at Prades, knew that there he could draw on the inspiration of his native soil. For although a voluntary exile from Spain, in Conflent he was in his Catalonian homeland.

As in the Catalan Pyrenees on both sides of the frontier, this culture was first expressed in a long series of Romanesque churches. To left and right as we go down the valley these include Oreilla, Evol, Thorent, Fuilla, Corneilla, Villefranche-de-Conflent, Fillols, Taurinya, the tower of Prades, Espira-de-Conflent, and Marcevol. (Note the *-lla* and *-ya* Catalan suffixes, which three centuries of *réunion* have failed to assimilate).

But up in Andorra or Tahull these Romanesque churches would still stand much as they were built. Their frescoes of the same early period, if these had survived, would have been bought by wealthy Barcelona and transferred to the Museum of Catalan Art on Montjuich. For once the tide of the Reconquest had flowed south, there were never again the resources to rebuild or embellish what the eleventh and twelfth centuries had erected.

Conflent, however, was lower and richer; and Aragonese expansion brought it nearer to the centres of Catalan power. In the fourteenth century this extended as far as Montpellier, and Perpignan became the capital of an independent 'Kingdom of Majorca'. And so, as in the provinces of coastal Catalonia, new churches were built; and these, and many of the older ones, too, were filled with paintings and sculptures.

The speciality of this art, which reached its height in the fifteenth century, was the retable or altarpiece. Within the Romanesque churches already mentioned examples can be seen at Evol, Corneilla, Prades, and Espira. There is some interesting fourteenth-century sculpture in Villefranche, and a seventeenth-century Crucifixion in Fillols. Amongst later churches the finest altarpiece is the seventeenth-century one of Serdinya, which also has three Catalan primitives.

Wherever there was a particularly dense flowering of some art form, it is worth asking whether there was not some particular local reason. The Gothic cathedrals of the Ile-de-France were inspired by Abbot Suger's work at St-Denis. The monuments of eighteenth-century Portugal owe much to the 'school' of artists and sculptors required to decorate the great abbey-palace of Mafra. For Conflent the *source de rayonnement* of its Romanesque art was St-Michel-de-Cuxa.

For in the spiritual and artistic revival of the Christian West after the year 1000, when the millennium which was to have heralded the Second Coming had passed without incident, and when the storm of Moslem aggression and Viking attacks had at last subsided, this monastery stood in a peculiarly pre-eminent position. Founded in 878 by monks who had been driven from further up the valley by one of the Tet's periodic yet unpredictable floods,* a century or so later it had attracted to its cells some outstanding personalities. They included St. Romuald, himself the founder of a religious order; Pietro Orseolo, the Doge of Venice who built St. Mark's; and Guarin, a friend of that interesting personality, Pope Sylvester II.

Guarin became Abbot, and, with his successor Oliva, was largely responsible for the abbey church. Its earliest parts, dating from 975, are not so much Romanesque as pre-Romanesque. In the transept can be seen 'horse-shoe' arches of 'Mozarabic' influence such as appear in the mosque (now the cathedral) of Cordova. A circular crypt built about the year 1000 to shelter relics brought back by Guarin from the Holy Land is supported on a single thick pillar in the form of a palm tree.

Vegetation rather than scripture was the inspiration, too,

* Some scholars believe these particular floods may have been caused by the bursting of the lakes which once stood on the upper Tet above Mont-Louis.

of the carved capitals of the cloister, which date from about a century later. Almost half of these, and of the rose-coloured marble pillars on which they stood, have been retrieved from the various private owners to whom they found their way after the abbey was sold at the Revolution. We therefore have a good idea of what it was like when complete.

But an even better idea can be had by visitors to the Metropolitan Museum of Art in New York, which has acquired an even larger number of the capitals and columns. As it is not the only such collection it has reassembled, it can readily be understood why it has been nicknamed 'The Cloisters'. One Pyrenean cloister has found an even more unsuitable home. For the *Sunday Telegraph* recently reported that Paradise Island in the Bahamas has 'Versailles Gardens, laid out in great terraces by Huntingdon Hartford, and theatrically crowned by a fourteenth-century French cloister transplanted from Montréjeau'.

I hope that you are as lucky as I in your guide round St-Michel-de-Cuxa. He was in his sixties, and obviously not a professional. He wore jeans, a dirty raincoat, and Catalan *espadrilles*. But his language and delivery were those of *France-Culture*, as he dwelt lovingly on almost every stone and statue. Only France could have produced him. And equally only a party of French tourists could have followed his every step and word for over two hours.

The attractions of Conflent are not limited to Romanesque architecture. There are, for example, the fortifications of Villefranche-de-Conflent, originally medieval and sixteenth-century, but restored and enlarged by Vauban before he set to work on Mont-Louis. Horticulturally the valley is almost as rich as the plain of Roussillon itself: in peaches more so. My memories of Prades are redolent of fruit and flowers.

In this respect Conflent makes an abrupt contrast with the deserted *pays* of Fenouillèdes immediately to the north. This is the only corner of the Pyrénées-Orientales where Catalan is not spoken. For this reason, and also because she went as far as Quillan and as far as Perpignan, I feel that Freda White ought to have covered this region which lies along the road between them. However, she did not; so we shall briefly visit it.

Arid *garrigue* or heath, it grows little except a wine similar to that of the Corbières hills further north. But as natural wonders it has the almost perpendicular gorges of the Agly river at Clue de la Fou and at Galamus. And for architectural and historical interest it contains a glorious series of ruined medieval castles.

Five of these: Olivier de Termes, Aguilar, Quéribus, Peyrepertuse, and Puilaurens, were known as the 'sons of Carcassonne', for they formed the outriders of that bastion in the defence of Languedoc when Roussillon was Aragonese. But there are others, amongst which Arques, Durfort, and the well-preserved Villerouge-Termenès are particularly worth a visit.

The fact that they all date from the twelfth and thirteenth centuries, and their connexion with Carcassonne, may lead readers to ask whether they played any part in the Albigensian wars. They did indeed. Raymond de Termes valiantly but unsuccessfully defended his castle against Simon de Montfort in 1210. And Quéribus survived as the last centre of open Cathare resistance for eleven years after the fall of Montségur.

Perched on its 'eagle's nest', it might have held out for many years longer; and the manner of its fall was a little sad. Olivier de Termes, whose name the castle of Termes now bears, belonged as we have seen to a family originally opposed to the invasion from the north. His uncle had even been a Cathare bishop. But he himself had become Catholic, and even accompanied his friend St. Louis on Crusade. He was used as a decoy to lure Chabbert de Barbera, the commander of Quéribus, into a trap. And Chabbert, in return for his release, ordered Quéribus to surrender.

The nineteenth-century English in due course discovered Conflent, just as they had earlier discovered so many unlikely places at the other end of the Pyrenees. Their centre here was Vernet-les-Bains, a spa set high above the right-hand side of the valley. As so often, its development as a British colony can best be studied not in any local documents, but in the archives of the London missionary societies.

Thus the Society for the Propagation of the Gospel was sending summer chaplains to Vernet from 1882 onwards. But it was not until the committee meeting of the Colonial and Continental Church Society on 18th December 1889 that the idea of a winter chaplaincy was even considered. And it was 19th April 1911 before Lord Roberts laid the first stone of the church of St. George, which was consecrated at the end of the following year.

The colony's progress from then onwards could have been dramatic. In 1913, after a leave from India spent at Vernet, V. C. Scott O'Connor published *Travels in the Pyrenees*, a work still on loan in many public libraries. Reading it one glimpses tweedy Georgians acclimatizing themselves to Europe after years overseas administering their vast Empire, which had so increased during the years since their more formal compatriots had established themselves at Pau. Walking across one of the loveliest public gardens in the Pyrenees, they had the use of the Casino during the winter months as a *club anglais*. But the flowering of this eastern Pau was cut short by the First World War. The marble monument erected to the Entente Cordiale in 1921 was the epitaph rather than the celebration of Scott O'Connor's 'Vernet of the English'.

The oblivion into which it had sunk by 1964 can best be gauged by a remark made to me then by my friend the Reverend Barnes, chaplain of St-Jean-de-Luz and all south-west France. 'You'll be surprised to hear that I've now got six churches to look after instead of only five. We've discovered a fine, well-built church at Vernet-les-Bains in the Pyrénées-Orientales. It's been closed and forgotten about for years.'

He gave me the name of the lady who had the key, and some weeks and several hundred kilometres later I called on her. The last representative of the colony, she had never lived in Britain herself, and for years had enjoyed few opportunities of speaking English. We found it easier to converse in French.

The colony has left one place-name behind it: the Cascade des Anglais beyond the Gorges of St-Vincent, formed by a stream which tumbles down from the last great mountain of the Pyrenees. For our compatriots knew what they were doing in choosing Vernet. It commands magnificent views of the great snow-covered pyramid of Canigou, at whose foot it lies.

What makes Canigou so impressive is the way that it rises ten miles north of the main chain, dropping swiftly to much lower ground on three sides. But on the fourth side it does not stand in quite such glorious isolation. For a line of eminences, only a little less than its 9,300 feet, runs south-west, connecting it with the frontier chain. This line forms the barrier between Conflent and Vallespir, and is crossed by only a couple of tracks. The hamlet of Mantet on one of these saw its population drop from seventy-nine in 1936 to a mere thirteen in 1962.

On a spur from this chain, and approached from Vernet by a different route from that leading to the peak itself, stands at 3,500 feet the Abbey of St-Martin-du-Canigou. Founded just after the year 1000 by Count Guifred of Cerdagne, who installed there a 'colony' of monks from St-Michel-de-Cuxa, it is slightly later in date than the older parts of the larger monastery. But its isolation, and the state of decay into which it had fallen even before the Revolution, give it an even more archaic air. This has survived its restoration as a retreat house since 1902.

The church is on two storeys, the lower of which, being beneath ground level on three sides, is generally described as a crypt. The cloister was also of two storeys. It has been restored so that three of its sides are of the original, plain, tenth-century design. The fourth, however, is composed of pillars from the vanished upper, twelfth-century cloister, with vividly-carved capitals.

Count Guifred, when he became a widower for the second time, himself entered the monastery he had founded. He even hollowed his own tomb out of the rock; and it can still be seen beside those of his two wives. His austere life here must have suited him, for he only died in 1056. And looking about him he must often have echoed the sentiments, and perhaps even the very words, of the old Catalan hymn:

> *Montanyas regaladas,*
> *Son las del Canigo,*
> *Que to l'estiu flaxeiren,*
> *Primaver' y tarder.* . . . .

> Delightful mountains,
> Are those of Canigou,
> Which flower in summer,
> Spring and autumn. . . .

4. VALLESPIR

Canigou is so central in the consciousness of French Catalonia because it is so central geographically. To reach Vallespir from Conflent we have to go right round it. It is unnecessary, however, to descend into the plain of Roussillon. For the last mountainous stretch of the *Route des Pyrénées*, the N618 we have met so often, joins the two valleys before running off, flat and straight, to the sea at Argelès.

It crosses an arid, deserted *pays* called the Aspre, not unlike the Fenouillèdes further north. At some distance up a track from it stands yet another example of Catalan early Romanesque: the priory of Serrabonne. The choir of its eleventh-century church is supported on arches in rose marble which were charmingly carved in the twelfth century with the stylized flora and fauna we met at St-Michel-de-Cuxa.

'Aspre', of course, is a local rendering of *âpre*, meaning harsh; and a deformation of the same word forms the second half of 'Vallespir'. But 'harsh valley' is no more correct as a description than is 'Greenland' of that grim Arctic territory.

At the beginning of this chapter I described how the four Catalan valleys we were about to visit offered surprising contrasts of climate. We have seen how the exposed, raw Capcir led to the southerly-facing, high but sunny Cerdagne, and then down to the sheltered, fertile Conflent. The Vallespir is even more favoured. For it is protected to the north by Canigou itself. And running as it does up to where the Pyrenees and the frontier dip away to the south, it is the southernmost region not merely of the department, but of France. Oranges grow in the open between Céret and Amélie-les-Bains.

Céret, the lowest town before the plain, is in fact better known for its cherries, although I have been unable to trace any derivation of its name from *cerises*. Alongside a modern bridge, the Vallespir's river, the Tech, is crossed by a fourteenth-century equivalent of Sidney Harbour Bridge or the Golden Gate. It throws a single elegant span a hundred and fifty feet long and half as high.

Half a mile separates the bridge from the main part of the town, where one still hears a lot of Spanish spoken by Republican exiles who have lived here since the collapse of the Catalan front early in 1939. Thirty years earlier another Spaniard had come there, seeking freedom and self-expression of a different kind. For to Céret in the early years of this century came not only Picasso, but all the masters of Cubism: Braque and Marquet amongst them. Max Jacob the poet also settled there, and gave the group a voice. After 1918, when these had moved on from Cubism, and away from Céret, they were succeeded there by other artists, such as Raoul Dufy.

The result is that the little Musée d'Art Moderne, in part of a former convent, is not only extraordinarily rich in the works of a long list of modern masters. It reflects also a side of them never glimpsed in the great impersonal galleries. Here, hung in pleasing informality, they show themselves off duty, *en famille* as it were.

For a family is very much what they must have formed at Céret. A letter from Cocteau here, a sly portrait by Picasso there, show the almost bantering intimacy in which they must have lived. Yet the line is right, the touch is sure, even in such trivia thrown off by the hand of genius.

Five miles up the valley lies Amélie-les-Bains. It received its name from Louis-Philippe's Queen Amélie, a contemporary of our William IV's Queen Adelaide, whom she resembled in self-effacing good nature. But its waters were known far earlier, as its still-used *Thermes Romains* testify. Without any particular monuments, it is an extremely pleasant and extremely French little place, with several good restaurants offering Catalan dishes prepared with Gallic *savoir cuire*.

The Tech is joined here by an affluent called the Mondony, which runs through a gorge immediately before it enters the town. The footpath which follows this forms one of the pleasant walks available to those staying in this driest and sunniest of spas.

The market town for Vallespir, however, remains Arles-sur-Tech, three miles up the river. The very earliest abbey in Catalonia was founded here, almost as soon as the Arabs had been chased out of the 'Gothic March', that corner of the old Visigothic kingdom which lay north of the Pyrenees. Rebuilt in 1046, it is a further variation on 'Roussillon Romanesque'. The pillars were duplicated a century later, the better to support the roof. The Gothic cloister, of a century later still, also has twin columns, but for reasons aesthetic rather than structural.

The most unusual details of the abbey are at the main entrance. The doorway itself belongs to the original Carolingian church, with a fine Romanesque Christ in majesty of the 1046 reconstruction above it. Also featured are the 'simiots', mythical beasts with the faces of monkeys and a taste for babies, from which Abbot Arnulf delivered the Vallespir in 960 by fetching relics from Rome.

Against a wall and behind an iron grill to the left of the doorway stands a fourth-century marble tomb. It is said to be always full of clear water, although there is no visible source of renewal. Not surprisingly, this water is claimed to possess miraculous properties: the baron whose tomb of 1204 is let into the wall behind had earlier been cured by them.

Like certain other churches we have visited, the abbey has a magnificent old organ. Its case is not as old as that of Condom (1605) or of St-Savin (1557). But it seems certain that it is a reconstruction in 1764 of elements of a far more ancient organ; and nothing has been done to it since. It is, therefore, ideal for playing seventeenth-century music; and on *France-Culture* I have heard some enchanting concerts of pieces Louis XIV must have been familiar with, played on the organ of Arles-sur-Tech.

The town's other church, St-Sauveur, the nave of which seems to be falling to pieces, has a fine Romanesque tower.

Those familiar with the overseas property advertisements of the 'serious' English Sunday newspapers will recognize the name on one shop-front as they go up the main street of Arles. It is *Midi Roussillon*, an enterprising little estate agency which has capitalized on Vallespir's sunny climate, and on the give-away prices of land on the stony *garrigue* of the Aspre, or in the mountain communes emptied by depopulation.

'Choose your own land . . . from 1 to 2,000 acres . . . at your own price: from 5 pence per square yard' reads one brochure before me. And in a Sunday newspaper as I write *Midi Roussillon* offers 'between Mediterranean and Pyrenees'—

17 acres evergreen oaks	FF 20,000 (£1,800)
24½ acres chestnut trees	FF 16,000 (£1,450)
Old farmhouse and 25 acres land	FF 56,000 (£5,000)
Sheepfold and 1¼ acres land	FF 19,000 (£1,700)

Apparently the greatest success has been achieved with Belgians seeking a haven for their capital on their return from the Congo. I wouldn't put anyone off such a purchase. Periodically the idea appeals to me too. But then with my self-contained motor caravan, and no doubt selfish self-sufficiency, I am well-equipped to make the most of twenty acres of evergreen oaks or chestnut trees. And the fact that even so I have not yet purchased them shows that there is something to be said against doing so.

For what constitutes the access to that old farmhouse? Are water and electricity laid on? If not, then how far off must the pipeline and the cable be brought? And what is the altitude of that otherwise so desirable sheepfold? The sense of these questions becomes apparent as we proceed beyond Arles up the valley.

For twelve miles there is only one hamlet; and the roads to left and right, leading to mountain villages in the foothills of the Pyrenees or of Canigou, are steep and narrow. (Amongst these villages Montferrer, Serralongue and Coustouges have good Romanesque churches.) The main road itself runs between forests of evergreen oaks and chestnuts—how would you feel all alone on twenty acres hereabouts?—and climbs even steeper after passing through a gorge. By the time we reach Prats-de-Mollo the valley is in truth a little *âpre*.

Prats-de-Mollo, however, will make us forget land-hunting for a while. It is a delightful little medieval town at two thousand five hundred feet, contained almost entirely within Vaubanesque ramparts. The church above the *ville basse* has a Romanesque tower, but was otherwise rebuilt in very late Gothic immediately after the French took over in the seventeenth century. Many of the streets, however, could still belong to Spain; and there is an ancient *Maison des rois d'Aragon*, where those kings used to reside when visiting their possessions north of the Pyrenees.

Appropriately, the ramparts are still pierced by a 'Porte de France' and a 'Porte d'Espagne'. A stiff climb from the latter can take one up to the thirteenth-century watchtower called the Tour de Mir, with its view of Vallespir from over five thousand feet.

The less energetic will be content to drive up to La Preste, a spa with monumental, rather barrack-like buildings at the very head of the valley. Here are treated such nasty-sounding complaints as *la colibacillose urinaire, d'autres suppurations urinaires, les petits signes du prostatisme,* and *la lithiase urinaire*.

Until 1964 Vallespir was for the motorist a cul-de-sac. But now a road runs from Prats-de-Mollo up to the Col d'Ares, and down to Camprodón and the road along the Spanish Pyrenees from Puigcerdá to Figueras. Many passes, set deep between mountains, or always lost in cloud, make poor viewpoints. But the Col d'Ares, at some five thousand four hundred feet, is not only high enough and exposed enough. It also has the clear skies of a Mediterranean province, and the dry air of Vallespir, to give those who pause there a panorama of both *la Catalogne* and *Cataluña*.

Chapter 8

ALONG THE GARONNE

1. LOMAGNE

We left the Garonne at Muret, on the battlefield which in 1213 sealed the fate of Languedoc. The old South-west: troubadours, courts of love, Cathares, and even the patois as a major literary tongue, went down before Simon de Montfort in a deeper and more durable sense than ever the 'Old South' went down before Grant and Sherman. Only today, after more than seven centuries as a distant town in a remote province, is Toulouse again rising towards metropolitan status.

The city itself has been described by Freda White in *West of the Rhône*. All that I shall add to her words is the shrewd remark of a recent French writer that it makes a better impression on first arrival than on closer acquaintance. Fortunately most readers will be there for hours rather than weeks, and can carry away a picture of mellow brick basilicas, the bustle and colour of the Place du Capitole, and all the bridges and quays of the Garonne and the Canal du Midi, without sensing an inner hollowness, nor the strains due to sudden expansion.

Its sudden expansion, and its rise towards metropolitan status, are alike caused by its emergence as an industrial centre. In part this has been due to a deliberate act of government, in its twin programmes of *décentralisation* and *régionalisation*. The aim of these is to avoid the France predicted by sociologists for the year 2000, divided between a vast conurbation around Paris, and *'le désert francais*'. But their viability in many peripheral provinces has yet to be proved.

Their outstanding success in Toulouse is due not only to the proximity of Lacq and Boussens, and of the lowest watershed between Mediterranean and Atlantic, to an ample supply of labour coming from the valleys and the *coteaux*, and to the climate, educational facilities, and lovely countryside offered to the necessary *cadres* or executives. It is due also to the vision of Marcel Dassault, the industrialist who built up Sud-Aviation.

He was not planting on entirely virgin soil. Readers of Antoine de St-Exupéry's *Vol de Nuit* will remember how Toulouse was the home-aerodrome of the French company pioneering an air-mail service to South America between the wars. Jean Mermoz, who first flew across the South Atlantic in both directions, was a well-known figure here. And Clément Ader, whose primitive *avion* of 1897 gave the French word for aeroplane, was born at nearby Muret. Moreover, the aviation industry tends to thrive in regions with little industrial background, like America's West Coast.

The airport of Blagnac, from which the French Concorde has risen on so many test flights, lies just off the road we shall follow along the left, 'our' bank of the Garonne. After several well-lost weeks in the Armagnac or the Pyrenees I have been brought abruptly back to the twentieth century by the sight of the hangars of Sud-Aviation, or by the landing of a BEA airliner from London. Thanks to the Concorde project, it is no longer Pau or Biarritz, but Toulouse which has the largest British colony in the south-west. Because it never formed part of the Plantagenet dominions (Henry II just failed to take it in 1159) it in fact has a larger English population today than at any time in its history.

A quiet detour would take us through Pibrac, a modern pilgrimage centre with considerable local influence. It stands beside the loveliest château of the Toulousain—Renaissance, but as wholly brick as the nearby city's Romanesque and Gothic basilicas.

And it is brick all the way as we follow the more direct route beside the Garonne. Nothing could be more *toulousain* than the octagonal tower of Grenade, whose borrowed name and regular street plan alike proclaim it a bastide. But on leaving Grenade we leave behind, if not the brick, at least the Toulousain as a province, to enter a delightful little *pays* called the Lomagne.

It consists of that part of Tarn-et-Garonne which lies south of the Garonne. Tarn-et-Garonne is a more than usually artificial department, with no historical unity, created by Napoleon in 1808 in order to give Montauban a prefect of its own. But Lomagne was a viscounty under the Dukes of Gascony as early as the tenth century. Like Grenade, its principal villages are often bastides, and almost always important markets.

For this is a rich countryside, full of fruit and poultry. We have left the dry, grudging Ariège, the *coteaux* with their need for a strictly delimited mixed farming, the sandy pinelands. 'The townships which mark the road from Agen to Toulouse preserve an age-old prosperity on the ancient route from the Mediterranean to the outer Ocean,' says one writer on this region. And the fact that Toulouse and Agen, and the road between them, lie on the other bank, makes the journey along quiet departmental roads on our own side all the pleasanter.

Verdun-sur-Garonne, the first place in Lomagne, gets its name from a Celtic prince called Virodunos, but had a *bastide* added in the thirteenth century. The two quarters are still joined together by a brick bridge.

Twelve miles north the eighteenth-century remains of the Cistercian abbey of Belleperche, now a farm, are again of brick. It was completely rebuilt in this later style after being sacked by the Protestants in 1572. These were commanded by a local enemy, the Baron of Terride, whose château had likewise to be restored after a siege in the same year.

The stalls of Belleperche abbey, together with a seventeenth-century Crucifixion, are in the modern church of Cordes-Tolosanes, a hamlet all by itself at the end of a lane, with an immense view across the river and over the plain between the Tarn and the Garonne. And all over Lomagne, especially at

31. The twin-columned Gothic cloister of the abbey of Arles-sur-Tech

32. The château of Labrède, family home of Montesquieu

Bouillac and Verdun, can be found treasures and sculpture from another monastery, that of Grandselve, which has completely disappeared except for its guesthouse.

Most attractive of the townships on the river itself is still-fortified Auvillar. Its name, from *altum villare*, means the high hamlet, and like Cordes-Tolosanes it commands a vast panorama. Its central 'square' is round, and so are the *cornières* or arcades which surround it. Two hundred years ago it owed its prosperity to pottery, and to a delightful industry of goose-quills for writing; and for long before that to the passing river boats, for whose sailors a second church was built down by the Garonne in the fourteenth century.

Auvillar was the birthplace cf Marcabu, one of the greatest troubadours. But the square fourteenth-century tower called the 'Château des Anglais' at Donzac five miles down the river, and the nearby bastide of Dunes founded by Saint Louis's brother Alphonse de Poitiers, remind us rather of the unhappier age of Anglo-French wars which followed. So do the crumbling fortified villages of Sérignac and Maubec, just off the N128 which bisects Lomagne on its way from Montauban to Auch.

On that same road lie Lazaret, whose château of the abbots of Belleperche, built in 1500, has a splendid staircase; and Beaumont-de-Lomagne, a bastide whose church was a cathedral in the fifteenth century, and which has choir stalls from the now vanished abbey of Grandselve. At Beaumont was born in 1601 the mathematician Pierre de Fermet, 'the real inventor of the differential calculus' according to Laplace. Pascal thought even more highly of him: 'Je vous tiens pour le plus grand homme du monde.'

The most interesting church of Lomagne belongs to a much later period. La Chapelle, eight miles south of Auvillar, was originally a Templars' oratory. But its restoration in 1776 gave it the air of a miniature Louis Quinze opera house, with decorations of the period, and with seats arranged in three tiers.

To the same century belong the châteaux of Lamotte-Bardigues near Lavit, and nearby Gensac, whose lady was accorded the honour of seduction by Henry IV. But the loveliest château in Lomagne is Gramat, on a side road to Lectoure. Built between the thirteenth and sixteenth centuries, it has one wing completely Gothic and one as uncompromisingly Renaissance, with a beautiful façade towards its gardens.

My own happiest memories of Lomagne, however, are centred on a much more recent if no less historical château. It is that of Monbrison, where Christian de Monbrison has established in the twelve hundred acres around his family seat the finest herd of cattle in France to be managed according to the precepts of organic farming. They live out in the fields all the year, and the hay and root-crops fed to them have been grown without chemical or artificial fertilizers. At first his peasant neighbours were scornful. But when they saw his cows resisting a hard winter better than their own they began to come to him for advice and help.

The really intelligent farmer is so often a man of wide culture. It is a delight to hear Christian de Monbrison giving his views on current developments in England, which he knows well; or telling how he would like to describe his experiments in a book modelled on the *Lettres Persanes* of Montesquieu, an earlier economist and agriculturalist of the Garonne. His family have always been innovators hereabouts: the château of St-Roch a couple of miles away, where his father lives, was rebuilt by them in the nineteenth century in the style of the châteaux of the Loire.

The two houses face each other in rolling country across a subsidiary stream, and Christian de Monbrison is not too fond of the less varied Garonne valley itself. But it is to the flattest part of that valley that we shall return to end our tour of Lomagne.

St-Nicolas-de-la-Grave stands in the angle where the river changes direction, opposite where it is joined by the swift Tarn below the great abbey of Moissac. Even our road along the left bank, therefore, leaves it to one side. There seems little going on, therefore, around the restored brick castle first built by Richard the Lion Heart, or in the lifeless streets.

Yet in one of its houses was born, on 5th March 1658, Antoine Lamoth-Cadilhac, who during his work of colonization in Canada and Louisiana founded the city of Détroit. He would be as surprised as I was to learn that he had given the last part of his name to the most famous status symbol issuing from the production lines of General Motors.

2. AGENAIS

We described the Lomagne as rich by comparison with some of the other regions we have explored. The only adjective for the Agenais is fruitful.

'Beneath a very mild climate, the valleys of the Agenais offer almost everywhere the perfect image of agricultural opulence . . . each township has its speciality. Around Port-Sainte-Marie the orchards of peach and cherry trees create at the beginning of spring, symphonies in rose and white, while the vines scale in regular ranks the north slope of the valley. . . . Around Marmande it is the tomatoes and the pumpkins which dominate. Near Agen the choice is better still: fields of artichokes, of lettuces and of asparagus at Brax and at Dolmeyrac; beds of onions, of garlic and of shallots at Layrac: borders of chicory, of asparagus and of aubergines at Bon-Encontre, of carrots, of leeks and of endives at Colayrac and at St-Hilaire'.

Although Brax and Layrac are the only places in this list to lie on our bank of the river, the writer's remarks apply equally well to that part of the Agenais lying south of the Garonne, which falls within our limits. He goes on to describe how all this produce finds its way 'towards Paris, where the sale of *agenais* early fruit and vegetables falls in the calendar between those of the Vaucluse and those of the Loire valley'.

In the calendar between Provence and the Loire is not really a very comfortable place to fall; and although its prunes, the famous *pruneaux d'Agen*, have become a household word, the district's lesser-known fruit and vegetables lack the recognition they deserve. But the French farmer in recent years has shown his initiative in fighting for a living. In Brittany he has blocked the high streets with artichokes or cabbages whose wholesale price he considered too low. In Roussillon he has halted the trains and lorries bringing competitive produce from Spain. In the Hérault he has even sabotaged wine arriving from Algeria.

The methods of the Agenais are milder, as befits its climate. Those crossing the departmental border of Lot-et-Garonne in full summer, enjoying yet suffering from that *grande chaleur du sud-ouest* which builds up after the end of June, may have encountered the same happy highwaymen who have more than once halted me.

Sometimes wearing an attempt at local costume, more often in everyday leisure clothes, they are the *Jeunes Agriculteurs* or Young Farmers of the department. Lean, brown lads, and well-made girls with a southern shapeliness lacking in the flat-chested Marianne, who always seems to be drawn from a north French model, they smilingly proffer peaches, pears, and inevitably prunes, and invite their captive to the makeshift lair they have erected beside the highroad.

There in heaps lie more fruits for the tasting; bowls of honey and of *foie gras* to smear on the chunks of fresh bread provided; wines of Buzet or of Cocumont—and perhaps even *armagnac*—to be *dégoûtés*. The charmed and replete prisoner continues on his way after release with a strong prejudice in favour of the *produits de qualité* of the Agenais, and of their so persuasive methods of marketing.

I myself always continue with something more substantial. For on such promotional occasions these products are offered at cost price. For those with enough space this is the opportunity to stock up with wine as cheaply as *chez le vigneron*; *pâtés* or cheeses as reasonably as if purchased personally at the *coopérative*; fruits and vegetables as inexpensively as if acquired *directs de l'agriculteur*. My memory dwells lusciously on trays of peaches which were still meltingly reminding me of the Agenais weeks later in Brittany —or even in Spain, where it was years before I realized that the *melocotones* I so often chewed as a dessert were in fact the same fruit.

A certain ripeness, such as accompanies the achievement of the *juste milieu*, flavours indeed all one's memories of this province.

For just as its *primeurs* reach Paris between those of Provence and of the Loire, so its scenery mingles a northern verdancy with southern fruitfulness. Historically, too, it has been a meeting-ground, although here the achievement of the *juste milieu* has not always been painless.

For the Agenais was a debatable land between French and English, as its many bastides such as Lamontjoie and Francescas testify. And it provided the headquarters for the two greatest leaders in the Wars of Religion which split the south-west a century after the last English had left.

The home of Blaise de Montluc, the Catholic commander, was the château of Estillac, five miles south of Agen. It stands very much as he rebuilt it in 1570, with its vaulted kitchens supported by columns. He still lies in the garden, beneath a recumbent statue in a white marble mausoleum. And within a few kilometres still stand also the churches of the neighbouring villages, which no doubt symbolized for him the faith he so cruelly defended: Romanesque Aubiac, with its doorway unusually cut into the tower, and archaic cupola above the choir; Moirax, even earlier, with an even stranger cupola; and Layrac, a pure creation of the Order of Cluny, consecrated by Pope Urban II himself in the same year, 1096, in which he launched the First Crusade.

Montluc was ruthless. 'He was a killer,' said Freda White to me. She has some good lines on his methods in *Three Rivers of France*. Yet he won the respect of the greatest of his opponents, who like Churchill praising the generalship of Rommel in the darkest days of the Second World War, spoke of Montluc's *Commentaires* as the 'Bible du soldat'.

It is strange how one good word can transform a character for us after four centuries, when it comes from Henry IV. He, too, spent much of his time in the Agenais. For Nérac, a mere ten miles as the crow flies from Estillac, was the administrative centre for that northern part of his family lands inherited from the Sires d'Albret. After the loss of Spanish Navarre it became an alternative, and in many says a preferable residence to the somewhat isolated château of Pau.

Here, then, with the Baïse offering a speedy route to the high-way of the Garonne, and with a choice of wines (and *armagnac*) beyond Jurançon, reigned the Court of Navarre celebrated by Shakespeare in *Love's Labour's Lost*. In such a setting it was French, rather than Spanish or even Pyrenean in feeling and two of the Queens who presided over it, Marguerite d'Angoulême and Marguerite de Valois, were indeed 'Princesses of France'.

Of the Renaissance château where this court was held, only one of the four wings survives. An octagonal tower encloses the staircase up to a charming open gallery, slightly protruding, which rests on convoluted pillars. This is now one of the quietest corners of a town never more than moderately busy. We can therefore the more easily imagine the scenes when the writer of the *Heptaméron* held court here, or when Catherine de Medici arrived in 1579, with her daughter, Marguerite de Valois, for a conference with Henry of Navarre, the latter's estranged husband. The conference was intended to end the war between Protestants and Catholics. (Catherine also brought her celebrated Flying Squadron, a 'fifth column' of noble young ladies of good looks and easy virtue.)

Just across the river lie formal public gardens, which I feel may well have formed part of the grounds which must once have surrounded the château. For a few years later the distant playwright was to set his entire action in a 'Park, with a Palace in it'.

The courtiers of Navarre lived too early to enjoy *pâté de foie gras*. This is first referred to as being served by an innkeeper called Taverne at Nérac towards the end of the seventeenth century. For it was only the introduction of maize from the New World which made possible the wonderful poultry of Gascony and Périgord.

But they must often have taken the walk along the Baïse known as the Garenne. It was already ancient then, as is shown by a Roman mosaic and a fountain erected by the Hospitallers of St. John. It was transformed into the shady promenade we know today by Antoine de Bourbon, the father of Henry IV.

The Vert-Galant himself often played there as a boy; and legend has it that it was the scene, too, of one of his earliest romances. It would certainly rank as the most bitter-sweet of them. It tells how at nineteen he seduced a young girl working in the gardens, who on being abandoned drowned herself in the Baïse. Henri was too tender a lover for his warm embraces to lead so abruptly to so cold a tragedy. But the story of Fleurette's death has given the excuse for a statue beside the Garonne by David Campagne, as beautiful and as haunting as that of the 'Little Mermaid' of Copenhagen, and for the equally haunting lines:

A peine ils s'étaient vus qu'ils s'aimèrent d'amour,
Elle comptait seize ans, lui trois de plus,
Ravie, Fleurette à cet amour donna sa vie;
Henri, Prince d'Albret, ne lui donna qu'un jour.

Later, as King of Navarre, he must often have strolled beside the Baïse discussing more serious matters with his advisers and lieutenants during the years when Nérac was his headquarters facing the Catholic armies to the north. For it was also a bastion of Protestantism, where Jeanne d'Albret welcomed Calvin. The house where he stayed is next to the Pont-Vieux, a sixteenth-century bridge which gives the best view of the oldest quarter of the town. Here, too, stands the house of the great Duc de Sully, who was to become so powerful and so competent a minister when *le meunier de Barbaste* had become *le roi de France*.

Barbaste lies four miles down the Baïse. But the wheels of the mill from which the royal 'miller' got his nickname are turned by its affluent the Gélise, which is crossed by a long Romanesque bridge. It is not of corn or flour that this 'loveliest fortified mill in France' reminds us, with its four six-storeyed towers and its austere high walls, but of the great spirit who could give such an unlikely setting an aura of the Parc aux Cerfs, and of the Hundred Years War when such a construction was necessary.

Nearby are other places to remind us of that struggle: the bastide of Vianne, complete with walls, towers, and four gateways; and the château of Xaintrailles, dominating this region from its hill, with its great square crenellated keep. Though showing traces of its twelfth-century origins, it was almost entirely rebuilt about 1440 by Poton de Xaintrailles, the friend of Joan of

Arc who ten years earlier had led the only attempt to rescue her.

As we noticed when visiting the Armagnac, the lands north of the Pyrenees retain a devotion to the Maid to this day. It was the murder of the Count of Armagnac by the Burgundians in 1418 which first turned the Gascon seigneurs against the English. But it was she who decisively won them over to France. The roll of her companions-at-arms reads like a gazetteer of the south-west: Coarraze, Verduzan, Barbazan, La Hire de Préchacq, Poton de Xaintrailles. . . .

Hereabouts *La Guerre de Cent Ans* is still *the* war. A friend of mine who lives at Barbaste has a cork factory two miles down the Casteljaloux road at Lausseignan, and claims that the name of this village means 'the bleeding' (*saignant*), and refers to some forgotten battle long ago between French and English. He may be right. For it was only thanks to him that I learned that George Sand stayed long periods at the house called Le Guillery two miles further on (it belonged to her first husband, the Baron Dudevant), and that she took the name of her book *La Mare au Diable* from the lake on private land on the other side of the road, two miles further still.

She only took the name, for the novel's actual setting is the open countryside of Berry, hundreds of miles to the north. La *Mare au Diable* is surrounded by pines, here mixed with the cork-oaks which gave my friend's father the inspiration for setting up his factory. For the road cuts across the north-eastern corner of the great pine-forest. Casteljaloux is a timber-town, redolent of resin and sawdust and newly-cut planks.

But in the Agenais the pines peter out well before the Garonne. The last commune of the Lot-et-Garonne on the river is Meilhan, on a little hill or *tertre* running steeply down to the canal which parallels it for much of its length, and links at Toulouse with the Canal du Midi. In visits to a friend there I have savoured much of the quality of life in these middle reaches of the Garonne: the beef of the 'Blonde d'Aquitaine' cattle which were first bred on its rich pastures; the wine from Cocumont where her sister teaches; the excellent lycée which she attended across the river at Marmande; and the patois which she understands, and which both her grandmothers still prefer to speak.

> *Abriù, quités pas un hiù.*
> *Maï, quito ço qué té plaï.*

(An *agenais* version of 'Ne'er cast a clout 'til May is out', adjusted by a month on account of the more favourable climate).

Even in this age of the internal combustion engine the waterway below remains central in the consciousness of those who dwell beside it. The canal runs higher than the river here, and great plane-trees at once anchor and disguise its dykes. It has brought those parties of foreign yachtsmen with whom my *agenais* friend spent such interesting evenings. And metaphorically at least it was 'down the river', even if she made the journey by road, that she travelled to complete her studies so brilliantly at the University of Bordeaux.

3. SAUTERNES

In making her journey from Meilhan to Bordeaux in search of higher education my friend was following a tradition not only ancient, but venerable. A thousand years before the Hundred Years War broke out, the same road was taken by the son of a doctor at Bazas, now a pleasant little town on the edge of the forest, with a former cathedral of every period from Romanesque to the eighteenth century.

It was a road which was to give him in the first place an outstanding professorial career at Bordeaux, before making him for a moment one of the most powerful men in that autumnal fourth-century world. For the prestige of Ausonius led the Emperor Valentinian to appoint him in 367 as tutor to his son Gratian, with the title of Questor of the Sacred Palace.

'The Sacred Palace' was as much an intricate hierarchy, a sort of movable Whitehall-cum-Pentagon, as an actual physical residence. In the later 360s it was situated at Trèves, a convenient place from which to watch the barbarian tribes in those nearby parts of Germany which Rome had never conquered. It lies at the heart of the 'hock'-producing vineyards, thus giving it at least one thing in common with Ausonius's native province. And he seems to have been happy there, writing poetry in praise of the Moselle valley, and of the leisured life of its villas, which has caused historians to postulate the late survival of a civilized 'pocket' in that oft-devastated frontier region.

But the percipient *bordelais* recognizes that in these poems 'In hymning the Moselle it is in fact the "blonde" Garonne which he evokes.' And when his native land is his actual subject, the ordered hexameters are suffused with a passion little less than Romantic. Bordeaux, then as now, is 'glorious by Bacchus . . . where the spring is long and the winter brief. . . . When the Ocean, father of waters, fills the estuary with his disturbed tide, one sees the whole sea together with its waves moving forward. . . . Bordeaux has my love, Rome my veneration . . . here is my cradle, there my curule chair.'

The 'curule chair' was no literary metaphor. On his pupil's accession as Emperor, the offices showered upon him included that of Prefect of the Gauls. This gave him supervisory powers over Spain and Britain, as well as over Gaul itself. And his family shared in his success. Within three years of this appointment they had acquired a wide variety of jobs—and of estates, too.

By the time he was deprived of office in 384, by Gratian's successor Theodosius, he himself owned no less than eight villas between which to divide his prosperous retirement. There were his town house in Bordeaux, and an estate in the suburbs; properties near Libourne, Saintes and Poitiers; others in Bigorre, and between the Bassin d'Arcachon and the Etang de Cazaux; and finally the family lands round Bazas. All were in the South-west. Half are well within the region covered by this book.

This accumulation has led some historians to conclude that Ausonius was just one more member of a greedy class of land-owners. But his love of the land, not only as a store of value but as a way of life, was genuine. Like many Roman writers of three or four centuries earlier, such as Pliny the Younger writing beside

Lake Como, he often expresses his taste for calm country life in preference to the hurry of the town. But in his case there was less reason why this should be a mere literary pose. Towns had shrunk during the troubled third century, drawing themselves within ramparts which enclosed but a fraction of their former area. Life was a meaner thing in fourth-century Burdigala, whose narrow streets already resembled the medieval Bordeaux where the Black Prince reigned as viceroy, than in the extensive, comfortable country villas of the Gallo-Roman aristocracy.

That Ausonius became so well-established a member of that aristocracy is less a criticism of him, than a compliment to a society which even in its late autumn could grant such rewards to its cultural leaders. Perhaps it unconsciously recognized their importance. For it was only in the fourth century that Latin at last superseded the Celtic and Iberian tongues of pre-Roman Gaul. Thenceforward there could be no effacement of the civilization still recalled by the routes along which it had travelled. For the Roman roads of the Gironde still bear self-explanatory names like 'Camin Rouman', 'Chemin Gallien', and even 'Chemin de la Vie'.

One facet of that civilization had taken root much earlier. Contrary to what one might suppose, this region, 'glorious by Bacchus', is not ideally suited to the vine. But soon after the Roman conquest, and the spread of Roman wine-drinking habits, the local landowners introduced from Albania a grape, the *biturica*, well adapted to their difficult climate of frequent rain, early frosts, and poor, sandy soils. Soon they were able not only to meet their own needs, but to open an export trade. Amphoras stamped with the name of one of the most active amongst them, M. Porcius, have been uncovered even at Pompeii.

The trade has never looked back, and over the centuries each corner of the region has developed its particular vines and processes. The family estates of Ausonius lay just outside what is now the Sauternes, a name with a flavour for all who have a taste for sweet white wines.

It is one of the most specialized, 'sophisticated' wines which exist. The grapes are picked one by one, as and when each reaches the required 'noble decay' which alone gives Sauternes its golden, almost cloying quality. A special fungus acts as the catalyst to induce this unusual degree of over-ripeness.

Of the five villages to whose territories the *appellation* is restricted, only Sauternes itself and Barsac (the interior of whose church has good eighteenth-century wood- and wrought iron-work) evoke an immediate response. Of the individual estates, Château Yquem is deservedly the best known. But it is the seventeenth-century Château de Malle which is most worth visiting for reasons architectural as well as viticultural.

This sandy countryside on the edge of the pinelands can be viewed as the cradle not only of Ausonius, and of a great wine, but also of the first of the Avignon popes. For it was Archbishop Bertrand of Bordeaux whom King Philip the Fair of France caused to be elected as Clement V in 1305, and who was only too willing that Cardinals and Curia alike should be transported north of the Alps.

For at Avignon he was within reach of his birthplace at Villandraut, nine miles west of Bazas. Here he built a vast rectangular castle. Its walls, crowned by six round towers, still stare across the deep ditch which formed the best protection in this flat landscape.

Even while he was dissolving the Order of the Knights Templar, causing their leaders to be burned and allowing kings everywhere in Europe to confiscate their lands on the excuse of their greed, he made ample provision for his own family. His nephews built castles for themselves on the same plan as Villandraut in a wide semicircle round that of their uncle: Budos, which was to endure a fierce siege by Henry V, Fargues, Roquetaillade, and la Trave.

This last lies on the road between two interesting churches: Romanesque Préchac with curious sculptures, and Gothic Uzeste where Clement V himself lies buried. Like Villandraut, la Trave stands beside the little Ciron, which runs through un-likely gorges deep in the pine forest before flowing through the Sauternes to join the Garonne.

Was it the example of Ausonius, the seed which he planted, which was long after to inspire two other *girondin* landowners to literary achievement? Or was this brought out by some quality in the common background of all three? François Mauriac, whose estates lay on the opposite bank to the one we are following, plumped for the environmental factor: 'La Garonne débordée roule en moi ses eaux comme de la terre liquide.' A very different writer, Anatole France, who was merely a visitor here, would have agreed with him: 'One must have been born beside the Garonne to be wise with that liveliness, and to give reason such a brilliance, common sense such fantasy.'

Certainly fantasy has seldom been more brilliantly tempered with common sense than in the *Lettres Persanes*. This 'most serious of frivolous books' is said to have been written by Montesquieu at Clairac in the Agenais, where he had an estate.

But he was born at Labrède, just off the main road from the Sauternes into Bordeaux. There is nothing frivolous about the books he wrote in the family château there, above all about the *Esprit des Lois*, which was almost the handbook of the moderate reformers who initiated the Revolution more than thirty years after his death in 1755. His library and bedroom are included in a tour of the château. With its thirteenth-century keep, fifteenth-century chapel, and uneven yet harmonious silhouette reflected in a wide moat, it would be worth visiting even if a genius had not lived and worked there.

Montesquieu's understanding of the political and social importance of commerce and agriculture came from experience. President of the Parlement or High Court of Guyenne at Bordeaux, he was able to observe the growth and operation of that great city's trade during its most prosperous century. As landowner he discussed their farming problems with his tenants in their own patois. And he shared with them the love of their own most important product—at Labrède no longer a *sauternes* but a *graves*. He even went so far as to say that he did not know if his wines owed their success to his books, or his books to his wines!

Envoi

ACROSS THE GARONNE

In 1588 Henry of Navarre rode north from Nérac to consolidate his victory at Coutras, and in due course to claim and win the throne of France. The family lands which had cradled, nursed, and so long sustained him: Albret, Marsan, Foix, Nébouzan, Gabardan, Soule, Basse-Navarre, Béarn, never saw him again. He probably never guessed that his departure was final. But it is tempting to wonder whether he gave a backward look as he crossed the Garonne, and whether it was one of those rare days when it is said to be possible to descry the Pyrenees from as far away as Agen.

Let us hope that we shall be luckier, and revisit the South-west many times. We shall find again all the qualities so well described by Freda White in her books on the neighbouring regions. At the end of the two later ones she commented on the changes she noted in French life during the years which had elapsed since the publication of *Three Rivers of France*. Since she last wrote, of course, there have been more changes still. A swift evolution is inevitable for a nation which seems set—with or without the ambitions of its leaders—to be the heartland of the new Europe.

Yet the links with the past remain unbroken in the lands north of the Pyrenees, even though the old provinces ceased to exist nearly two centuries ago, and though the factories rise around Lacq and Toulouse. They live not only in the old stones of church and château and in the Occitanian tongues which even as they die determine the way French will be spoken here, but in the very minds of the people.

I can best illustrate this by the two 'pop' songs which I heard most frequently as I was preparing this book. One, with the title and refrain *P'tite anglaise*, had a stanza which drew the maximum of erotic pathos from that most classic of all conflicts, the Hundred Years War. It even evoked Joan of Arc at the stake to add poignancy to a twentieth-century love affair.

The other had a simpler, time-honoured theme. It told how the singer saw a girl beside a laurel tree, where she was looking after her sheep, and how later at the village fair he arranged to meet her 'up on the hill'.

Je l'ai vue près d'un laurier, ell' gardait ses blanches brebis . . .
A la foire du village un jour je lui ai soupiré . . .

Then came the chorus, to a boisterous tune, telling how he followed her instructions, plucking a posy of eglantine and whistling for her up on the hill. But he went on whistling, he went on waiting . . . she never came.

Ell' m'a dit d'aller siffler là-haut sur la colline,
De l'attendre avec un petit bouquet d'églantines
J'ai cueilli des fleurs et j'ai sifflé tant que j'ai pu
J'ai attendu, attendu, ell' n'est jamais venue

I remember hearing it fairly shouted one night by a café full of young men at l'Hôpital-St-Blaise, and thinking that its sentiments were not far removed from those of Cyprien Despourrins or of Gaston Phoebus (see page 68). Surely England can only gain from a closer association with a land whose pop-stars still chant of shepherdesses and village fairs?

APPENDIX

I. GETTING THERE

As indicated in the Introduction, two main roads from Paris lead straight to the heart of our region: the N10 via Bordeaux, and the N20 via Toulouse. Two main railway lines run almost parallel with these, and are served by two famous trains: the *Sud Express* and *Le Capitole*. The first of these, on the flat, straight track across the empty Landes, reaches the highest speed attained by any regular passenger train outside Japan.

The main lines fan out towards termini far up a number of Pyrenean valleys. The range itself can thus be reached by train almost as easily as when Belloc was writing in the early years of this century.

Elsewhere in the region, however, French Railways have carried out severe rationalization. The quaint *chemins de fer départementaux* have been everywhere swept away. And the bus services which at first replaced them have suffered the same curtailment as in Britain with the spread of 'personal transport'. Nor are the infrequent services which survive exactly cheap.

'Personal transport' is therefore the ideal method of touring this region. All categories of roads are everywhere excellent, if occasionally narrow as they wind over the hills (as in going against the grain' over the switchback *coteaux*). And this quality of French roads can transform the journey to and from the region. it is possible to avoid altogether the N10, the N20, and any other

M   *177*

main highways, following for hundreds of miles almost equally direct *routes départementaux* across Poitou or the Sologne.

For a through route, on the other hand, which is blessedly quiet, hitch on to the N140 which from Figeac on the Lot winds through the Limousin uplands and across Berry all the way until it joins the N7 beyond the Loire.

The journey there and back can indeed give you some of the best moments of your holiday, especially if you prepare for it with the three great books of Freda White.

By air, direct flights to the region are operated by BEA to Biarritz, Bordeaux and Toulouse, and by Aer Lingus to Tarbes-Lourdes.

For all information on communications, as well as on hotels and restaurants, consult the French Government Tourist Office at 178, Piccadilly, London W1V OAL.

2. SETTLING THERE

Our great-grandfathers knew what they were doing in establishing British colonies at Pau, Biarritz, St-Jean-de-Luz, Arcachon and Vernet-les-Bains. Climatically (together with, of course, the Vallespir) these are the most favoured areas, with a milder, if a damper climate than the Côte d'Azur, and with no Mistral. But make allowance for the rain. After seven happy years some friends of mine were driven away from their lovely home near Pau by rheumatism.

Do not underrate, either, the advantages offered by the proximity to what may at first sight appear the pathetic vestiges of those colonies. An occasional service in the Anglican church, an occasional cup of tea in the adjoining library with a little English conversation, can make a welcome change, however much you may now yearn for total immersion in *la civilisation française*.

The library is a particularly important lifeline. For you will find yourself enjoying as never before the beauties of the English language, when no longer daily reminded of its banalities and degradations.

English newspapers can only be bought all the year round in Biarritz, St-Jean-de-Luz, the Gare Internationale at Hendaye, Pau, Bordeaux and Toulouse. And they cost more than twice the already high price they have reached in Britain. So remember that the *Daily Telegraph* and *Sunday Telegraph* (Circulation Department, 135 Fleet Street, London EC4) have a particularly efficient and inexpensive overseas subscription service. The *Daily Telegraph* has even organized especially for readers in France a bulk air freight service to Paris, and on by post.

If you choose to live elsewhere in the region you will require, as an absolute necessity, fluent French or the determination to acquire it. And you must expect spells of very cold weather. I have spent bitter January nights even in the Garonne valley. But you will have your own good reasons for what you are doing, and you will have all the opportunities for reducing your cost of living afforded by purchase of milk, wine, fruit and vegetables straight from the producer.

British estate agents have so far confined their attentions to the region of the *Three Rivers*; and I have run across only one couple—in Armagnac—who have embarked on that 'doing up' of old farms and cottages which is already a favourite English pastime in the Dordogne. So establish your own local contacts—and take your time before you buy.

An unexpected experience made me think that a short note on settling in the region might be of some use. When I was working on the Basque Coast in the late 'fifties and early 'sixties I often visited the library beside the Anglican church in Biarritz on a Thursday afternoon. There, making a social occasion out of the weekly ritual of changing their books, was most of what was left of the local British colony. As I enjoyed the best cup of tea to be found between Dover and Gibraltar, and listened to accounts of the colony's plusher pre-war days, I used to wonder how long it could survive in even this attenuated form.

After giving up my work I was not again in Biarritz on a Thursday until 1969. Doubtfully I approached the Rue Broquedis, and was quite surprised to find the library open, and the tea party in full swing as usual. But what surprised me most of all was that I knew no one there. My ten or so friends of a decade earlier had died or moved away. But they had been replaced by ten or so new 'Anglo-Saxons' who had moved into Biarritz in the intervening years.

3. EATING AND SLEEPING

Three local styles of cooking make the Pyrénées-Atlantiques, with the Chalosse immediately to the north of it, one of the important gastronomic regions of France.

The *cuisine basquaise* you may best remember for its piquant *pipérades* of carefully-cooked peppers, tomatoes and onions; and for its chickens bathed in well-seasoned tomatoes.

The *cuisine béarnaise*, apart from its celebrated sauce, is most typically represented by the *garbure*, 'that thick cabbage soup, in which the serving spoon should stand up unsupported in the pot ... there is nothing like stirring it with a leg of *confit d'oie*, while it simmers on the fire, and, when one's fingers get too hot, letting this unctuous extremity slip into the skilfully-savoured soup, on which swim buttered and cheese-toasted crusts'.

The *cuisine landaise*, with its *hauts-lieux* at Hagetmau and Amou, is the realm of rich poultry in all its forms, from the succulent *poulets des Landes* to the various preserved members of the ducks and geese which their mistresses have so industriously *gavés*, and on to the crowning glory of *confit de foie gras d'oie*.

You will eat well throughout the region, even outside this favoured corner, though such areas as the Agenais, Armagnac and Ariège make no claims beyond those of fulfilling any trencherman's dreams. Specialities include in the extreme west the oysters of Arcachon; and in the east the several varieties of the bean-based stew called *cassoulet*. That 'de Castelnaudary' is with reason generally regarded as the best. And in Pyrenean Catalonia the *cuisine catalane*, always more appetizing than in Spain, can now also claim to have survived in a purer form than on the Costa Brava.

Appendix

In the Médoc and the Sauternes the region produces some of the world's great wines. But it also produces a great deal of eminently drinkable *vin ordinaire*, and outside the larger towns and the resorts this is almost invariably included automatically as part of the menu. The Garonne marks fairly exactly the line south of which the welcome litre of *rouge* appears without comment on the table, and without mention in the bill. Here again our region now has an advantage over Spain.

Hotels are almost everywhere, and of every kind. Lists giving prices and facilities are available from the French Government Tourist Office, 178 Piccadilly, W1V OAL. Those to ask for are 'Aquitaine' and 'Midi-Pyrénées'.

The FGTO can also supply the booklet entitled *Gîtes de France*, giving details of simple furnished accommodation made available by countryfolk. This scheme has particularly caught on in some of the more remote departments, like Ariège, where isolated farmers enjoy not only the supplement to their cash incomes, but the social contact with strangers.

Another more recent venture of this kind is 'Camping à la ferme', where farmers receive up to five tents or caravans at a time. They are bound to provide a supply of running water, and rudimentary toilet facilities. Invariably they are also only too pleased to supply milk, eggs and so on at producer's prices.

More ambitious, and slightly different in concept, are the 'Villages verts de vacances', rural communities which by laying on sports, entertainments, and so on during the summer months are trying to launch themselves as minor inland resorts.

4. MAPS

Michelin sections 71, 78, 79, 82, 85, 86.
Shell 'Cartoguides' No. 12, Pyrénées—Côte Basque, and No. 13, Languedoc—Roussillon.

BIBLIOGRAPHY

Fortunately no English writer has chosen to cover exactly the same region as that of this book, which has been deliberately set within the limits laid down by Freda White. The range itself has never been described better than by Hilaire Belloc in *The Pyrenees* (Methuen 1909), nor more imaginatively than by J. B. Morton in *Pyrenean* (Longmans, 1938). Wider areas are included in two of Nina Epton's wonderful books: *Navarre* (Cassell, 1957), and *The Valley of Pyrene* (Cassell, 1955). For the Pays Basque Rodney Gallop's *A book of the Basques* (Macmillan, 1940) remains essential. Much of the region is also described in:

South from Toulouse by Andrew Shirley (Chatto and Windus)
Gascony and the Pyrenees by John East (Johnson, 1970)
Road to the Pyrenees by Roger Higham (Dent, 1971)

But of course the British were writing about the Pyrenees, near which so many of them elected to live, long before the last few years. This has enabled Jacques Duloum, in his major work *Les Anglais dans les Pyrénées et les débuts du tourisme pyrénéen* (1739–1896) (Les amis du Musée Pyrénéen, 1970) to survey not only British achievements in exploring the range, and the history of the British residential colonies, but also the whole compass of British literary activity in these fields during the eighteenth and nineteenth centuries. Henceforward this will be required reading for the specialist.

Bibliography

Desmond Seward has recently published a scholarly and readable biography of Henry of Navarre under the title *The First Bourbon* (Constable, 1971).

The general reader will enjoy the regional surveys by teams of scholars published by Horizons de France: *Visages du Pays Basque* (1942); *Visages de Gascogne et de Béarn* (1948); and *Visages de la Guyenne* (1953) (although only about a third of Guyenne lies within our region). As the dates of publication indicate, these are becoming a little out-of-date, and a welcome awaits the Larousse series, *Découvrir la France*, when it gets round to the south-west. Highly readable, its presentation is nearer to that of journalism; and its somewhat unwieldy format may be the necessary quid pro quo for its fine coloured illustrations.

The central province of the region is beautifully evoked by Joseph de Pesquidoux in *La Gascogne* (Artaud, Grenoble).

As Freda White remarked, there are few histories to bridge the gap between those of France as a whole, and the perspective-deprived researches of local amateurs. But the 'Que sais-je?' series includes two useful little paperbacks: *Histoire de la Gascogne* by Charles Dartigue (Presses Universitaires de France, 1951), and *Histoire du Béarn* by P. Tucoo-Chala (Presses Universitaires de France, 1962).

Finally, *La Lomagne* has been covered from both the historical and the artistic viewpoints by the Chanoine Pierre Gayne of Campsas, in a short work which M. Ferlin of Montauban was kind enough to lend me when it was still only in typescript form.

INDEX

Adour, river, 17, 26, 30, 32–4, 36, 39, 75, 90, 95–7, 102–3, 105, 110–11, *Pl 19*
Ainhoa, 23
Aire-sur-l'Adour, 95–6
Albret, 47, 103, 105, 165, 175
Aldudes, les, 38–9
Amélie-les-Bains, 72, 154–5
Amou, 96, 180
Andernos, 106
Andorra, 47, 128–9, 139, 147
Arcachon, 105–6, 178
Arcangues, 29
Ares, Col d', 157
Argelès-Gazost, 72, 115
Ariège, river, 124, 128–34, 138
Arize, river, 135–6
Arles-sur-Tech, 155–6, *Pl 31*
Armagnac *eau-de-vie*, 79–81, 88, 90, 164
Arthous, abbey of, 48
Ascain, 23, 30
Aspe, valley of, 52, 65–75
Aspin, Col d', 118

Aspre, 153, 156
Aubisque, Col d', 71, *Pl 22*
Auch, 91–2
Aude, river, 16, 133, 137, 140–141
Aulus-les-Bains, 127
Aurensan, 88, 96
Ausonius, 169–71, 173
Auvillar, 161
Ax-les-Thermes, 130–1, 137, 138
Aydie, 76

Bagnères-de-Bigorre, 73, 111, 115
Baïse, river, 90, 94, 166–7
Barbaste, 167–8
Barbazan, 72, 122, 168
Barèges, 73, 115
Barsac, 172
Basques, 16, 21–45, 87, *Pls 3, 5*
Bassoues, 83
bastides, 48, 51
Bayonne, 22, 23, 32–6, 105

Bazas, 169–70
Béarn, 16, 32, 37, 40, 46–78, 109–10, 175, *Pl 4*
Beaumont-de-Lomagne, 161
Béhobie, 21, 26
Belleperche abbey, 160
Belloc-St-Clamens, 95
Bellongue, la, 125
Bernadotte, Jean, 61–2
Bétharram, 112, 113, *Pl 20*
Bethmale, 126
Biarritz, 22, 23, 25, 27–9, 178–180
Bidache, 40, *Pl 7*
Bidart, 23, 25
Bidassoa, river, 17, 21, 26, 33
Bielle, 70–1
Biert, 127
Biscarosse, lake of, 104
Bouillouses, lac des, 142
Boulaur, 93
Bourg-Madame, 145
British residential colonies, 22, 50, 62–5, 73, 105–6, 111, 114, 150–2, 159, 178–81, 183

Cambo-les-Bains, 31, 72
Canigou massif, 74, 152–4
Capbreton, 33, 105, 106
Capcir, 139–43
Capvern, 72, 110
Carla-de-Roquefort, 135
Carlitte massif, 140, 143–6
Casteljaloux, 168
Castillon-en-Couserans, 126
Cathare heresy, 47, 48, 123, 124, 126, 131, 132, 134, 137–138, 150, 158
Caumont, château de, 93
Cauterets, 115–16
Cerdagne, 143–7, 153
Céret, 154
Charlemagne, 38, 42, 67
Chioula, Col de, 138
Ciboure, 25, 26–7
Cintegabelle, 133
Coarraze, 60, 168
Cocumont, 164, 168
Comminges, 16, 66, 118, 120–4, 126
Condom, 80–3, 155
Conflent, 141, 146–54
Cordes-Tolosanes, 160–1
Cordouan lighthouse, 107
Corneilla, 147–8, *Pl 28*
Couserans, 16, 123–7

Dax, 49, 72, 95, 97
Despourrins, Cyprien, 67–8, 176
Donézan, 137–8

Eaux-Bonnes, 71, 73
Eaux-Chaudes, 73
Eauze, 80, 83
Escaladieu, abbey of, 110–11
Estillac, 165
Etigny, Intendant Baron d', 36, 91–2, 119
Eugénie, Empress, 27–9, 73

Fanjeaux, 134

Fenouillèdes, 149–50, 153
Flaran, abbey of, 84–5
Fleurance, 83, 91, 94
Foix, 132, 145, *Pls 26, 27*
Foix, county of, 16, 37, 47, 48, 53, 59, 124, 128–38, 175
Fontestorbes, 138
Font-Romeu, 143–4
Formiguères, 140

Galamus, 150
Garde, Pierre de la, 85
Garlin, 76–8
Garonne, river, 15, 16, 17, 21, 90, 114, 119, 121–3, 133, 158–73, 175, 179, 181
Gascon language, 35, 59, 89
Gascony, 16, 32, 47, 48
Gaston 'Phoebus', 53–4, 68, 76, 110, 132, 176
Gaube, lac de, 116–17
Gavarnie, 117–18, *Pl 24*
Gers, river, 91–2, 94
Gimone, river, 90, 92, 93
Gimont, 93–4
Gironde estuary, 103, 106–8
Gramat, 162
Grenade, 90, 160
Guétary, 23, 25

Hagetmau, 96, 180
Hasparren, 31, 36
Hastingues, 48, *Pl 6*
Hendaye, 21, 25, 26, 30
Henry of Navarre (Henry IV of France), 16, 28, 37, 40, 49,
51–2, 57–60, 67, 73, 103, 110, 165–7, 175, 184
Henry II Plantagenêt, 34, 47, 159
Hix, 145
Hôpital d'Orion, 54
Hôpital-St-Blaise, 44–5, 54, 56, 176
Hossegor, lake of, 104, *Pls 15, 16*
Hourtin, lake of, 104, 106
Huchet, Courant d', 104

Isle-en-Dodon, l', 90, 93

Jeanne d'Albret, 49, 58, 167
Joan of Arc, 34, 42, 81–2, 86, 167–8, 176
Jurançon, 59–60, 75

Kakouetta, gorges of, 43

Laas, 50, 113
Labrède, 173, *Pl 32*
Labrit, 101, 103, 105
La Chapelle, 161
Lacq, 55, 56, 159, 175
Lamarque, 108
Landes pine-forest, 15, 28, 32, 89, 98–103, 107, 177, *Pls 14, 15*
Lannemezan, plateau of, 90–2
Larrau, 43–4
Larressingle, 82, *Pl 12*
Laruns, 70–1
Latour-de-Carol, 146

Index

Lavardens, 82, 83, 86
Lavédan, 115–16
Layrac, 163, 165
Lectoure, 83, 94
Léon, lake of, 104
Lescar, 47, 55–6, 75
Lescun, 69, 71, Pl 11
Lesparre, 107
Lespugne, Venus of, 92
Llivia, 145–6
Lló, 145
Lombez, 90, 93
Lombrive, 131
Louhossoa, 32, 36
Louis IX (St. Louis), 47, 130, 132, 150, 161
Louis XIV, 26, 58–9
Lourdes, 61, 71, 111–14
Luchon, 73, 91, 119–20
Luz, 116–17
Luzenac, 128

Maladeta massif, 114, 119–20, 125
Margaux, Château, 107–8
Marguerite d'Angoulême, 56, 67, 83, 166
Martres-Tolosanes, 113, 122
Mas d'Azil, le, 135–6
Massat, 127
Masseube, 86, 90, 91
Mauléon-Soule, 41
Mauvezin, 110, 111
Meilhan, 168–9
Miélan, 83, 90, 94–5
Mimizan, 105

Mirande, 83, 94, 95
Mirepoix, 133
Monbrison, 162
Monein, 55
Montalivet, 103–4, 106
Montaner, 75–6
Mont-de-Marsan, 102
Montesquieu, 162, 173
Montesquieu-Volvestre, 136
Mont-Louis, 141–2, 144, 146, 149
Montluc, Blaise de, 165
Montréjeau, 95, 122, 149
Montsaunès, 122
Montségur, 131, 137–8, 150
Morlaas, 64, 75
Muret, 47, 123, 158, 159

Napoléon I, 28, 31, 42, 62, 160
Napoléon III, 27–8, 100, 112
Navarrenz, 51–2
Nay, 60–1, 66, 91
Nebouzan, 47, 92, 175
Néouvielle massif, 74, 118
Nérac, 59, 165–7, 175
Nive, river, 17, 30–3, 38, Pl 2
Nivelle, river, 17, 29, 33

Odeillo, 142, 144
Olivier de Termes, 150
Oloron, 46, 52, 53, 70
Oô, lake of, 119
Orthez, 53–5, 58, 62, 75, 97, Pl 10
Ossau, valley of, 52, 65–75
Oxocelhaya caves, 39

Pailhès, 135
Pamiers, 15, 132–3
Parentis-en-Born, 105
Pau, 46, 50, 55–65, 66, 110, 165, 178
Pauillac, 107–8
Peyrehorade, 48, 97, 118
Peyresourde, Port de, 118, 120
Pibrac, 159
Pic de la Sagette, 73–4
Pic du Midi de Bigorre, 114–15, 118, *Pl 21*
Pic du Midi d'Ossau, 70, 74–5
Planès, 142
Pointe de Grave, 106
Pompey, 16, 120
Port, Col de, 124, 127, 128, 131, 139
Portet d'Aspet, Col de, 125
Pourtalet pass, 66, 69, 74–5
Prades, 147–9
Prats-de-Mollo, 157
Préchacq, 97, 168
Preste, la, 157
Protestants in south-west France, 49–50, 57–8, 76, 136
Pyla, dune of, 106, *Pl 17*
Pyrenees, 15, 17, 65–75, 95, 114–20
Pyrénées, Parc National des, 74
Pyrénées, Route des, 71–2, 118, 123, 125, 126, 127, 131, 153, *Pl 23*
Pyrenees, Treaty of, 26, 139, 141, 145–6

Quéribus, 150
Quérigut, 137–8

Rhune, la, 24, 30, 74
Rieux, 123
Roland, Pas de, 31–2
Romans in south-west France, 16, 49, 92, 118, 120–2, 145, 169–71
Romieu, la, 84
Roncevaux, 37, 38, 44, 66, 67
Roquefort, 101–3
Roussillon, 16, 139, 141, 147, 149–50, 165
Russell, Count Henry, 114, 117

Saillagouse, 145
St-Aventin, 118
St-Bertrand-de-Comminges, 16, 56, 92, 120–2, *Pl 25*
St-Etienne-de-Baïgorry, 39
St-Gaudens, 95, 122
St-Girons, 123, 125, 126
St-Jean-de-Luz, 22–9, 64, 178, *Pl 1*
St-Jean-de-Verges, 132, 135
St-Jean-Pied-de-Port, 37–8, 40
St-Lizier, 124–5
St-Martin-du-Canigou, abbey of, 152–3
St-Michel-de-Cuxa, abbey of, 148–9, 153, *Pl 29*
St-Nicolas-de-la-Grave, 162
St-Palais, 40
St-Sauveur, 115
St-Savin, 116, 155

St-Sever, 91, 96–7
St. Vincent-de-Paul, 98
Ste-Engrâce, 43–4
Ste-Mère, 82
Salat, river, 124–7
Salau, 126
Salies-de-Béarn, 49–50, 72, *Pl 8*
Samadet, 87, 95, 113
Sand, George, 116, 168
Santiago de Compostela, pilgrimage to, 37–8, 44, 52, 69, 117
Sarrance, 67
Sault, 16, 137–8
Saurat, valley of, 128
Sauternes wine, 171–3, 181
Sauveterre-de-Béarn, 50, 53, *Pl 9*
Save, river, 90, 92–3
Sègre, river, 141, 143
Serrabonne, 153
Sévignac, 75
Simon de Montfort, 47, 123, 132, 150, 158
Simorre, 90, 91, 93
Socoa, 24
Solférino, 100
Somport pass, 16, 44, 48, 52, 66, 69, 117
Sorde l'Abbaye, 48
Soulac, 106
Superbagnères, 120

Tarascon-sur-Ariège, 131
Tarbes, 109–10
Tardets, 41

Tech, river, 16, 154–7
Terraube, 82
Tet, river, 16, 141–2, 146–9
Tillac, 82, 83, 94–5
Toulouse, 15, 128, 133, 158–9, 175, 177–9
Tourmalet, Col du, 115, 118
Trois-Villes, 42
Tursan, 95–6

Ustaritz, 30–1
Uzeste, 172

Valcabrère, 121
Vallespir, 147, 152–7, 178, *Pl 30*
Vals, 133
Verdon, le, 106
Verdun-sur-Garonne, 160–1
Vernet-les-Bains, 150–2, 178
Vianne, 167
Vicdessos, 131
Vieux-Boucau, 33, 105
Vignemale, 117
Villandraut, 172
Villefranche-de-Conflent, 147–149

Wellington, Duke of, 17, 33–4, 53, 59, 62–3
White, Freda, 15, 17, 48fn, 59, 77, 133, 135, 137, 139, 149–150, 158, 165, 175, 178, 183, 184

Xaintrailles, 81, 167–8